T0002231

To:

....

From:

....

Date:

....

BLESSED IS SHE

Who Hopes

Rae Simons

BLESSED IS SHE
Who Hopes

DEVOTIONS & PRAYERS
FOR WOMEN

BARBOUR
PUBLISHING

© 2023 by Barbour Publishing, Inc.

Print ISBN 978-1-63609-491-5

Adobe Digital Edition (.epub) 978-1-63609-629-2

All rights reserved. No part of this publication may be reproduced or transmitted for commercial purposes, except for brief quotations in printed reviews, without written permission of the publisher. Reproduced text may not be used on the World Wide Web.

Churches and other noncommercial interests may reproduce portions of this book without the express written permission of Barbour Publishing, provided that the text does not exceed 500 words or 5 percent of the entire book, whichever is less, and that the text is not material quoted from another publisher. When reproducing text from this book, include the following credit line: "From *Blessed Is She Who Hopes: Devotions and Prayers for Women*, published by Barbour Publishing, Inc. Used by permission."

Scripture quotations marked msg are from *THE MESSAGE*. Copyright © by Eugene H. Peterson 1993, 1994, 1995, 1996, 2000, 2001, 2002. Used by permission of NavPress Publishing Group.

Scripture quotations marked niv are taken from the Holy Bible, New International Version®. niv®. Copyright © 1973, 1978, 1984, 2011 by Biblica, Inc.™ Used by permission. All rights reserved worldwide.

Scripture quotations marked nlt are taken from the *Holy Bible*. New Living Translation copyright© 1996, 2004, 2015 by Tyndale House Foundation. Used by permission of Tyndale House Publishers, Inc. Carol Stream, Illinois 60188. All rights reserved.

Scripture quotations marked kjv are taken from the King James Version of the Bible.

Scripture quotations marked esv are from The Holy Bible, English Standard Version®, copyright © 2001 by Crossway Bibles, a publishing ministry of Good News Publishers. The esv® text has been reproduced in cooperation with and by permission of Good News Publishers. Unauthorized reproduction of this publication is prohibited. All rights reserved.

Published by Barbour Publishing, Inc., 1810 Barbour Drive, Uhrichsville, Ohio 44683, www.barbourbooks.com

Our mission is to inspire the world with the life-changing message of the Bible.

ecpa Member of the
Evangelical Christian
Publishers Association

Printed in China.

Introduction

We often think of hope as a cheery, optimistic outlook on life. The biblical concept of hope is far greater and deeper, though. It is a joyful and confident expectation that God not only has the future in His hands, but that He also has abundant blessings in store for us. We cannot know what the future holds, but we *can* know, without a shadow of a doubt, that the same God who was with us yesterday will be with us tomorrow—and forever.

We sometimes let ourselves be robbed of the joy and confidence God wants us to experience. We may feel as though the future is empty and barren. But hopelessness is always a lie, for our God has big plans for us! No matter how hard the road, it always leads us into His presence. We can face the future with joy, and as we do, we open ourselves to a deeper understanding of what God is doing in our lives. As we grow closer to Him, our hope will grow too—and we will be blessed.

Good News

The Spirit of the Sovereign LORD is on me, because the LORD
has anointed me to proclaim good news to the poor. He has
sent me to bind up the brokenhearted, to proclaim freedom for
the captives and release from darkness for the prisoners.

ISAIAH 61:1 NIV

Sometimes, some of us seem to forget that the Bible brings us *good news*. We allow ourselves to be burdened with depression and frustration; we wear frowns more than smiles. Others watching our faces and hearing our words might not be able to tell we have something special in our lives. In fact, they might think we feel pretty much like the rest of the world often does—hopeless. In reality, the Bible has given us the best news ever: we are unconditionally loved and made whole for eternity; and so, even when the world seems the darkest, we have hope!

SOVEREIGN LORD, REMIND ME THAT FROWNS, GLOOMY
ATTITUDES, AND ANGRY WORDS ARE NOT WHAT IT TAKES
TO DRAW PEOPLE TO YOU. HELP ME TO CHANGE THE WORLD
WITH THE GOOD NEWS OF THE HOPE I HAVE IN YOU.

Say Yes!

"I am the Lord's servant," Mary answered.
"May your word to me be fulfilled."
Luke 1:38 niv

When the angel came to Mary with the news that she was to give birth to God's Son, she didn't say, "Aw shucks, I'm just not good enough, Gabriel." She simply said, "Yes"—and her *yes* allowed a brand-new reality to be born into our world.

The word *yes* can have the same power in our lives. It's not always easy to say, though. We are often so aware of our own limitations that we lack the confidence to say yes to God. We look around and see all the reasons why saying yes to God would make no sense (it would cost too much money; people might think we were being silly; we don't have time; we're not good enough, smart enough, or popular enough). Mary could easily have said, "But I'm not married. And I'm too young. I'm not important or wealthy or powerful." Instead, she apparently didn't even ask any questions. She just said yes—and her *yes* brought hope to us all.

GIVE ME THE COURAGE, LORD, TO SAY YES TO HOPE—YES TO YOUR LOVE, YES TO YOUR POWER, AND YES TO YOUR WILL.

Patient Hope

*If we hope for what we do not yet have,
we wait for it patiently.*

ROMANS 8:25 NIV

Hope is a form of patience that shines with confidence. It's not the kind of patience that just plods along wearing a dreary face, putting up with life's troubles with big sighs and no expectation that anything better will ever come along. Instead, hope *knows* that something better is up ahead. Hope believes God will keep His word. Even though right now things may look frightening or sad, hope shines its light into our hearts, reassuring us that better times are yet to come. We can't see the future—but we believe God has amazing things planned.

DEAR GOD, WHEN I FEEL LIKE GIVING UP, GIVE ME NEW HOPE IN YOUR PROMISES. FILL MY HEART WITH JOYFUL EXPECTATION OF ALL YOU WILL DO BOTH IN MY LIFE AND IN THE WORLD. AND PLEASE, HELP ME TO BE PATIENT!

There's No Such Thing as "Hopeless"!

"What do you mean, 'If I can'?" Jesus asked.
"Anything is possible if a person believes."
MARK 9:23 NLT

Do you ever find yourself throwing up your hands and saying, "It's hopeless!" A painful situation you've struggled to improve may be frustrating you. It could be that you've tried to learn a new skill, and it's just not coming easily. Or maybe it's a person in your life who seems hopeless to you because no matter how many times they promise to change, they always fall back into the same hurtful behaviors. Everything is possible with God, but our own attitudes can get in the way, hindering the Spirit's movement in our lives and in the world around us. Things may not work out exactly as we hoped or as quickly as we wished—but with God, nothing is hopeless!

JESUS, THE NEXT TIME YOU HEAR ME SAYING I
THINK SOMETHING IS HOPELESS, REMIND ME THAT
THROUGH YOUR POWER, ANYTHING IS POSSIBLE.

Desperate Times

Make the most of every chance you get. These are desperate times!
EPHESIANS 5:16 MSG

We might read this verse and think to ourselves, *If things are so desperate, what's the point of trying? I might as well give up.* But that attitude can keep us stuck in old habits. It can also contribute to our world staying stuck in the old habits of violence, racism, and cruelty. There is an opportunity to find the good in every difficult situation. That's the attitude the apostle Paul is talking about in this verse from his letter to the church at Ephesus. There are opportunities for God's grace even in the most desperate times.

HOLY SPIRIT, I KNOW YOU ARE ALWAYS WORKING IN THE
WORLD. REMIND ME THAT EVEN THE MOST CHALLENGING
SITUATIONS ARE FILLED WITH UNSEEN POTENTIAL. WHEN
I ENCOUNTER CIRCUMSTANCES THAT SEEM HOPELESS,
GIVE ME THE HOPE I NEED TO ACT ON YOUR BEHALF.

Dare to Dream

"I will pour out my Spirit on all people. Your sons and daughters will prophesy, your old men will dream dreams, your young men will see visions."

JOEL 2:28 NIV

We sometimes think that dreams are impractical, a waste of time, but hope and dreams go hand in hand. Hope, like dreams, requires a sense of vision. In most cases, that doesn't mean God will send us into a trance where we have the sort of revelation He gave to the apostle John when he authored the book of Revelation. We can't literally see into the future. But hope gives us the ability to *imagine* a better future—and imagining something is the first step toward creating something new.

What dreams do you have? What may God be calling you to imagine for the future?

LORD OF POSSIBILITY, MAY I DREAM YOUR DREAMS FOR THE WORLD. GIVE ME A VISION OF YOUR KINGDOM, AND MAY MY DREAMS AND VISION GIVE ME THE COURAGE AND THE HOPE I NEED TO DO THE WORK YOU CALL ME TO DO.

Feed My Lambs

When they had finished eating, Jesus said to Simon Peter, "Simon son of John, do you love me more than these?" "Yes, Lord," he said, "you know that I love you." Jesus said, "Feed my lambs."

JOHN 21:15 NIV

Peter had failed Jesus miserably when he publicly denied knowing Him. Afterward, Peter must have wondered if Jesus would ever be able to feel the same about him. But Jesus did not criticize or scold Peter; He didn't ask Peter to try to do better in the future or embarrass him in front of the other disciples. Instead, Jesus talked to him one-to-one. First, He asked Peter to reaffirm his love—and then He told Peter to act on behalf of others.

Jesus still uses the same approach with each one of us. When we've failed Him, we often feel ashamed; we may want to give up trying. But Jesus doesn't want us to wallow in our shame and sadness. Taking action, getting involved, reaching out to those in need, and serving Jesus by loving others—that's how we regain our sense of hope and energy.

JESUS, WE BOTH KNOW HOW MANY TIMES I'VE FAILED YOU AND HOW HOPELESS AND POWERLESS THAT CAN MAKE ME FEEL. BUT I DO LOVE YOU. SHOW ME YOUR "LAMBS" WHO NEED MY HELP. RESTORE MY HOPE IN YOU.

The Courage to Hope

I eagerly expect and hope that I will in no way be ashamed,
but will have sufficient courage so that now as always Christ
will be exalted in my body, whether by life or by death.

PHILIPPIANS 1:20 NIV

During the 1930s, Dorothy Thompson was an American journalist who was one of the first people to speak out against Hitler and his Nazis. She took a stand for what she knew was right. She understood that courage wasn't the absence of fear, but that it was the willingness to face any circumstance with boldness and faith in the truth.

The apostle Paul also had the courage to know that everything—even death—can be meaningful; even the worst situations are opportunities to allow Christ to use us and fill us with His Spirit. We often do not understand why certain circumstances are allowed to happen, but in Christ, we can still have hope in a better tomorrow.

CHRIST JESUS, GIVE ME THE COURAGE I NEED TO HOPE EVEN WHEN I DON'T UNDERSTAND WHAT IS HAPPENING, AND MAY MY HOPE GIVE ME THE COURAGE I NEED TO TAKE A STAND FOR YOU.

Keep on Trying

We confidently and joyfully look forward to sharing God's glory. We can rejoice, too, when we run into problems and trials, for we know that they help us develop endurance. And endurance develops strength of character, and character strengthens our confident hope of salvation. And this hope will not lead to disappointment. For we know how dearly God loves us, because he has given us the Holy Spirit to fill our hearts with his love.

ROMANS 5:2–5 NLT

Two thousand years ago, the apostle Paul understood that seemingly hopeless situations can help us grow when we have the right attitude. If we continue to persevere and have hope, we can create something incredible! Perseverance—when we keep trying despite difficulties, opposition, and even failure—can make us stronger, more hopeful people. As Christ's followers, we have a hope that will never let us down or disappoint us, because our hope is rooted in God's love, a love that will never fail us. As we act in that hope, who knows what seemingly impossible things we may accomplish?

GOD OF LOVE, THANK YOU THAT YOU WILL NEVER DISAPPOINT ME OR LET ME DOWN. GIVE ME THE HOPE IN YOU THAT I NEED TO KEEP TRYING, EVEN IN SITUATIONS THAT FROM MY PERSPECTIVE SEEM HOPELESS.

Dreams

*"I, the LORD, reveal myself to them in
visions, I speak to them in dreams."*
NUMBERS 12:6 NIV

Do you have dreams for the future? If you do, are they wispy figments of
your imagination, fantasies to while away the boredom of sleepless nights
or a long car ride? Do you dismiss them as "castles in the air," with no
foundation in reality? Or do you take your dreams seriously?

The Bible goes so far as to say that God speaks to us through our
dreams. We often dismiss verses like that as referring to the sort of mys-
tical visions that only the old-time saints had; but the next time you find
yourself daydreaming about the future, listen for God's voice. What might
He be calling to you through your dreams?

GOD OF DREAMS, REMIND ME THAT YOU ARE ALWAYS SPEAKING TO
ME IN COUNTLESS WAYS I OFTEN OVERLOOK. TEACH ME TO LISTEN
FOR YOUR VOICE SO THAT YOU CAN LIFT ME UP ABOVE THE CLOUDS
AND GIVE ME A GLIMPSE OF YOUR VISION FOR MY LIFE. GIVE
ME HOPE FOR THE FUTURE THAT HAS ITS FOUNDATION IN YOU.

Keep Hoping

Even when there was no reason for hope, Abraham kept hoping.
Romans 4:18 nlt

Abraham and Sarah had had a long life together, but they had never had children. When Sarah was far too old to give birth to a child, Abraham would have been sensible to give up all hope of having a family. But he didn't. He was not some starry-eyed fanatic, living in an unreal world of wishes and make-believe. He and his wife lived down-to-earth lives filled with the practical challenges and limitations of desert life two thousand years before the time of Christ. He understood the facts—that his wife was too old to get pregnant—but he also believed God's promise to him.

Our situations today may also be filled with the disappointments of real life. We must face those disappointments, not wish them away. But all the while, our hope is in the Lord.

GOD OF SARAH AND ABRAHAM, THANK YOU THAT YOU ALWAYS KEEP YOUR PROMISES. MAY MY HOPE IN YOU HOLD FIRM, NO MATTER WHAT THE CURRENT CIRCUMSTANCES MAY BE.

Wait and Watch and Work

Let perseverance finish its work so that you may be
mature and complete, not lacking anything.
JAMES 1:4 NIV

Waiting, watching, and working is what the Bible refers to as "perseverance." It is not always easy to await the fulfillment of our dreams, but we know that they will come to pass in God's way and His timing when our hope perseveres.

It's the visible demonstration of our invisible hope in God. Even though we may not be able to see more than one step ahead, we take that next step—and then we do it again and again and again, one step at a time. As we put our hope into action, we begin to change inside. God uses our perseverance to transform our hearts. And then one day, we look around and realize the dawn has come.

GOD OF HOPE, GIVE ME STRENGTH TO KEEP GOING EVEN
WHEN I CAN'T SEE WHERE YOU'RE LEADING ME. MAY I
DO YOUR WORK AS I WAIT AND WATCH FOR YOU. MAY
MY PERSEVERANCE HELP ME TO GROW IN YOU.

Hope That Takes Action

Act on what you hear!
JAMES 1:22 MSG

Again and again, the Bible describes a practical hope, not a pie-in-the-sky, wish-on-a-star fantasy, but a real-life goal that requires our engagement and action with the world around us. True hope is acting in faith according to God's Word and what He's calling us to do.

Bible scholars aren't positive who wrote the book of James—he may have been the brother of the apostle John or he may have been Jesus' half-brother—but clearly, this long-ago author understood that spiritual hope takes concrete action in the real world. He challenges us to give our bodies as well as our souls to God. "Don't just offer thoughts and prayers," he says, in effect. "Get out there and do something practical."

SHOW ME, LORD, THE POSSIBILITIES YOU HAVE IN MIND FOR MY LIFE AND FOR THE WORLD AROUND ME—AND THEN GIVE ME THE COURAGE AND STRENGTH I NEED TO TAKE ACTION.

Make Up Your Mind!

But Daniel was determined not to defile himself by eating the food and wine given to them by the king.

DANIEL 1:8 NLT

Like you and me, Daniel lived in a society that did not honor God. He did not hide himself away from that society but was actively engaged in its politics—and at the same time, he did not allow anything to weaken his relationship with God. He did not consume the things this broken society considered nourishment. Instead, he received his sustenance from God, and as a result, God used Daniel to reveal Himself.

We can learn from Daniel's example. God wants us to bring His hope to our broken world, just as Daniel did to his; but we can't do that if we've "consumed" too much of our society's thoughts and attitudes. Mother Teresa once spoke of lamps only burning if you consistently filled them with the oil they needed, and the same is true of our hearts. If we want to shine with hope, we need to feed ourselves with prayer and time spent with God. We can't keep hope lit with only our society's empty promises.

FAITHFUL GOD, THANK YOU THAT I CAN COUNT ON YOU, JUST AS DANIEL DID SO LONG AGO. AND LIKE DANIEL, I'VE MADE UP MY MIND: ONLY YOU CAN TRULY SATISFY MY LONGINGS. ONLY YOU CAN KEEP THE FIRE OF HOPE BURNING BRIGHTLY IN MY HEART.

Only God

Yes, my soul, find rest in God; my hope comes from him. . . . He is my fortress, I will not be shaken.
Psalm 62:5–6 niv

It's all too easy to depend on things this world has to offer, things like money, houses, relationships, and professional roles. None of those things are bad in and of themselves; they are all gifts from God. But they are shaky resting places for our souls.

Hope is where our souls can truly rest. First, however, we must figure out where our hope is found! Ask yourself: Where am I resting my soul? What gives me hope? What holds me steady and keeps me safe? Am I living inside the fortress of my hope in God—or am I only admiring it from a distance?

LORD, I KNOW YOU ARE THE SOURCE OF ALL HOPE. NOTHING ELSE IN LIFE IS STRONG ENOUGH TO HOLD ME SAFE AND SECURE. WHEN I ASK MYSELF WHAT GIVES ME HOPE, IT'S YOU AND ONLY YOU.

Spring Is in the Air

*"The flowers are springing up, the season of singing birds
has come, and the cooing of turtledoves fills the air."*
SONG OF SOLOMON 2:12 NLT

We all have times in our lives when it seems winter will never end. Whether it's emotionally, spiritually, financially, or physically (or all four), life seems bleak and cold. We feel as though Narnia's White Witch has cursed our life, making it always winter. But just as Aslan brought spring to Narnia, so God will always bring new life to our hearts and circumstances.

We can expect that God will bring His promises to pass because it is what He reveals to us in His Word. We will not always be in a dry season but will soon see the rain of His blessing and favor in the form of answered prayers. Don't give up hope. Winter always comes to an end.

LORD GOD, GIVE ME HOPE EVEN WHEN THINGS SEEM HOPELESS.
FILL ME WITH EXCITEMENT AND EXPECTATION AS I WAIT FOR WHAT
YOU WILL DO NEXT IN MY LIFE. EVEN AS I SHIVER IN THE COLD,
MAY THE FIRST BREEZES OF YOUR SPRINGTIME WARM MY HEART.

Hope in the Darkness

The light shines in the darkness, and the
darkness can never extinguish it.

JOHN 1:5 NLT

The world is a wondrous place—but it is also filled with terrible things: hatred and war, cruelty and intolerance, suffering and death. We can't pretend those things don't exist, and the Bible never asks us to. Instead, the Bible assures us that God's light never stops shining, even in the darkest corners of our world.

To paraphrase South African theologian Desmond Tutu, there is hope when you can look into darkness and still find a source of light. Tutu had seen hope in the long night of his nation's apartheid, and that hope had burst into brilliant light when apartheid finally came to an end. This is the sort of hope that only Christ can give us, a shining hope that helps us see the Spirit's presence and potential even in the world's darkness.

CHRIST JESUS, WHEN EVERYTHING AROUND ME SEEMS
DARK, SHINE THE LIGHT OF YOUR HOPE INTO MY HEART.
MAY MY LIFE BE A LENS FOR THAT LIGHT, SENDING
HOPE OUT FROM MY HEART INTO THE WORLD.

The Giver of Gifts

Remember the wonders he has done.
1 CHRONICLES 16:12 NIV

When I was young, my head stuffed full of romance novels, I believed I could never be truly happy until I fell in love. I often gave up hope, but eventually, I did fall in love and get married. As it turned out, married life wasn't all romance like in the novels. Now, though, I longed for a baby—and then, after my first child was born, I started hoping we could buy our own house. . .and then a bigger house. . . Each time my hopes were satisfied, my attention shifted to the *next* thing I wanted. And each time, I often despaired of my hopes ever being granted.

Remember, everything you treasure now was something you once only hoped for! When we feel hopeless, longing for something that still lies ahead, we need to remember what God has already given us. As we fully enjoy the wonder of His gifts today, we will find our hope in the future restored. Who knows what God will do next?

LORD, I KNOW YOU HAVE MANY MORE GIFTS TO GIVE ME
IN THE FUTURE, BUT TEACH MY GREEDY HEART TO BE
HAPPY WITH WHAT YOU HAVE ALREADY GIVEN ME.

Hope That Leaps

Be joyful in hope, patient in affliction, faithful in prayer.
ROMANS 12:12 NIV

Martin Luther, the great Protestant reformer of the sixteenth century, once said that everything that is done is done because of hope. Think about it: Would you bother even getting up in the morning if you didn't have hopes for the day ahead? Would you pray, go to work, go to church, get married, have children, get a puppy or a kitten, plant a garden, remodel your house, or even have your hair cut in a new style if you had no hope?

According to Etymologeek.com, the words *hope* and *hop* come from the same ancient root, indicating that *hope* is an energetic sort of thing, something that allows us to leap forward into the future (even when we must do it step by patient step). Hope in God has the power to sustain us with joy even when life is hard, and it will give us the energy we need to be faithful and patient, praying and acting today to build a better tomorrow.

LORD, INSPIRE ME TODAY WITH YOUR HOPE.
MAY I LEAP PRAYERFULLY AND PATIENTLY INTO
THE FUTURE YOU HAVE PLANNED.

The Power of Praise

When they had sung a hymn, they went out to the Mount of Olives.

MARK 14:26 NIV

Because of hope, we set goals for the future. Hope also keeps us motivated as we work toward those goals. But how do we find the energy to get started when we know what lies ahead will be challenging, perhaps even painful?

Jesus knew the answer to that question. When He was soon to face His death on the cross, He took time to sing a hymn with His friends. He knew that praising God in song can strengthen our hearts and give us the hope we need to walk into the future, even when it's hard to face. We see this same truth revealed in the Old Testament too, when Judah's army was led by singers praising God before a battle. (See 2 Chronicles 20.) Praise shifts our focus away from difficult circumstances and allows us to see God more clearly. With our hearts fixed on God, we will have the hope we need to set off on our journey of faith, no matter what lies ahead.

GOD, WHEN MY HEART FAILS ME AS I FACE SOMETHING PAINFUL UP AHEAD, REMIND ME TO PRAISE YOU IN SONG. LIFT MY HEART WITH YOUR JOY SO THAT I HAVE THE COURAGE I NEED TO GET STARTED, KNOWING THAT THE ROAD, NO MATTER HOW ROUGH AND FULL OF SHADOWS, WILL LEAD ME HOME TO YOU.

God Won't Give Up

I am certain that God, who began the good work within you, will continue his work until it is finally finished.

PHILIPPIANS 1:6 NLT

We human beings are easily discouraged. God has done so many wonderful things for us in the past, and yet sometimes our hearts tell us that there's nothing left to hope for. We act as though the God who was able to get us through every challenge we've experienced so far has now somehow become too weak or too distant or too uncaring to help us. We're tempted to throw up our hands in despair and give up.

The apostle Paul knew, though, without any doubts at all, that the God who has been working in our lives ever since we were born will never stop working. With that assurance, we can pray for courage even when we are in despair. God is not limited by our thoughts and feelings, and He will give us the strength we need to keep going.

GOD OF YESTERDAY, TODAY, AND TOMORROW, THANK YOU THAT YOU NEVER GIVE UP ON ME. I KNOW I CAN FIND IN YOU EVERYTHING I NEED TO FOLLOW YOU, EVEN WHEN EVERYTHING I SEE SEEMS HOPELESS.

Pressing On

*I don't mean to say that I have already achieved these things
or that I have already reached perfection. But I press on.*
PHILIPPIANS 3:12 NLT

Jonas Salk, the man who developed one of the first successful polio vaccines, once spoke of hope being found in the dreams of those with the courage to turn them into their realities. Dr. Salk began to work on his vaccine in 1947, but it took eight long years before it was released to the public. During that time, he must have had many setbacks, days when his own mistakes and wrong turns might have tempted him to despair. And yet he pressed on.

None of us is perfect; we all get confused sometimes. Sometimes we even fall flat on our faces. Hope, however, is what keeps researchers like Salk working to find cures for deadly illnesses. Hope is also what kept the apostle Paul going as he spoke and wrote about Christ, despite his own failures and flaws. And hope is what can also get you and me back up on our feet when we stumble, so that we can press on toward the plan Christ has for our lives.

DEAR JESUS, YOU KNOW I'M FAR FROM
PERFECT—BUT MY HOPE IS IN YOU.

It's a Brand-New Day

Great is his faithfulness; his mercies begin afresh each morning.
LAMENTATIONS 3:23 NLT

Sometimes getting up to face a new day is a joyful moment; our courage and hope are high, and we feel confident that the day ahead will be a wonderful one. Other mornings, though, we have to work hard to muster up the courage and hope we need to face another day. We have all had those mornings when simply getting out of bed seemed to be a courageous feat. Maybe yesterday wasn't so great, and we fear another day that's just as bad (or maybe even worse). Maybe we really messed up things yesterday, and today we must face the consequences of our actions. Still, no matter what yesterday was like, here's the good thing about God: He gives us a new beginning every morning. No matter how bad yesterday was, we can have hope today. God's faithfulness and mercy are always ready to start fresh.

GOD OF MERCY, THANK YOU THAT EACH DAY IS A
BRAND-NEW HOPEFUL OPPORTUNITY TO SERVE YOU, TO GET
TO KNOW YOU BETTER, AND TO REJOICE IN YOUR LOVE.

Gratitude

"It never occurred to them to say, 'Where's GOD, the God who got us out of Egypt, who took care of us through thick and thin, those rough-and-tumble wilderness years of parched deserts and death valleys?'"

JEREMIAH 2:6 MSG

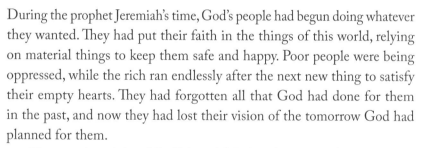

During the prophet Jeremiah's time, God's people had begun doing whatever they wanted. They had put their faith in the things of this world, relying on material things to keep them safe and happy. Poor people were being oppressed, while the rich ran endlessly after the next new thing to satisfy their empty hearts. They had forgotten all that God had done for them in the past, and now they had lost their vision of the tomorrow God had planned for them.

Have you lost sight of God's hope? Maybe it's time you looked back at your life and spent some time thanking God for everything He has done. Gratitude can restore your hope.

LORD OF LOVE, WHEN I START TO FEEL HOPELESS, REMIND ME TO THANK YOU FOR ALL YOU HAVE ALREADY DONE IN MY LIFE.

Joyful Hope

I will be filled with joy because of you. I will
sing praises to your name, O Most High.

PSALM 9:2 NLT

Sometimes it seems as though we can't possibly be happy when so much in our lives is uncertain. We don't know how we're going to find enough money for all the financial demands that lie ahead. We don't know what the future holds for our children. We don't know if we'll be able to spiritually, physically, and emotionally rise above the challenges of growing older. We don't know the answers to our world's enormous problems (like racism, poverty, and war). Amid so many questions that make us feel vulnerable and anxious, how can we even dare to be happy?

We can trust that when God is the source of our hope, we can live without knowing all the answers. A life of hope is also a life of joy.

GOD, YOU ARE THE SOURCE OF MY LIFE AND MY ONLY TRUE
SATISFACTION. EVEN WHEN I FEEL ANXIOUS ABOUT THE FUTURE,
PLEASE FILL ME WITH YOUR HOPE. MAY YOUR JOY LIVE IN MY
HEART, AND MAY I SHARE IT WITH EVERYONE I ENCOUNTER.

Hopeful Love

Love never gives up, never loses faith, is always hopeful, and endures through every circumstance.
1 Corinthians 13:7 nlt

Have you ever caught yourself saying to your spouse or a friend, "You *always*...!" Or "You *never*...!" Overgeneralizations like these put the other person in a box. They imply that the person is hopeless, bound to repeat the same terrible offenses, while never learning to do better.

When you say something is hopeless, you are saying there's no room for God to work in the other person's life. True love, the sort of love described in 1 Corinthians 13, is not so easily discouraged. It keeps believing the best of the other person. It endures the challenges of hurt feelings and irritation. That doesn't mean, of course, that we should put up with abuse; God wants us to protect ourselves and set healthy boundaries. But when we're talking about the ordinary selfish or careless failures, of which we're all guilty, love keeps plugging along. It has faith in the other person. It never gives up hope.

FORGIVE ME, LORD, FOR THE TIMES WHEN FRUSTRATION OR HURT HAS MADE ME IMPATIENT WITH A LOVED ONE. REMIND ME THAT I TOO AM FAR FROM PERFECT. THANK YOU THAT YOUR LOVE NEVER GIVES UP ON ME, AND TEACH ME TO LOVE MORE LIKE YOU.

Humble Hope

Listen for GOD's voice in everything you do, everywhere you go; he's the one who will keep you on track. Don't assume that you know it all. Run to GOD!

PROVERBS 3:6–7 MSG

Often, when we find ourselves losing hope, the reason is this: we've been depending too much on our own strength and intelligence. Instead of relying on God's Spirit to work in and through us, we've been taking pride in our ability to "go it alone." The wise author of Proverbs, however, reminds us that God is the one who keeps us on track. In order to hope in God, we must also think about God. We must make a habit of mentally paying attention, listening for God's voice, moment by moment throughout our lives.

MAY I HAVE THE HUMILITY I NEED, LORD, TO PLACE MY HOPE IN YOU RATHER THAN IN MY OWN ABILITIES. IN THE MIDST OF MY BUSY LIFE, KEEP MY THOUGHTS FIXED ON YOU.

The Source of All True Hope

Let your unfailing love surround us,
LORD, for our hope is in you alone.

PSALM 33:22 NLT

We cannot rely on any of the circumstances around us, including our jobs, our relationships, our bank accounts, and our reputations, to give us the kind of hope we need to face all of life's challenges and pain. We need something bigger than this world to anchor our lives.

Often, when people talk about hope, what they're referring to amounts to nothing more than flimsy wishes. Real hope always comes from God. It lives in our hearts and minds, unshaken by the world around us because it relies on nothing except God's unfailing love.

FAITHFUL LORD, TEACH ME TO PLACE ALL MY HOPE IN YOU.
THANK YOU THAT YOUR LOVE WILL NEVER LET ME DOWN.

Vision

Where there is no vision, the people perish.
PROVERBS 29:18 KJV

The long-ago author of Proverbs knew that we needed to be able to see past our present circumstances in order to keep going. Without those glimpses of a better tomorrow, we would give up. George Washington Carver, the early twentieth-century scientist and inventor, echoed the wisdom from Proverbs when he said that there is no hope without vision.

Born into slavery and denied the education white children received, Carver committed his life to Jesus when he was a young boy, and his faith never let him down. His certainty that God loved him gave him the confidence he needed to pursue education and then use his education to help others. He believed that God would reveal great things to him if he simply put his trust in the Lord. This was the vision that gave him hope in the endless possibilities God created. And this is the same vision that will fill our own lives with joyful hope.

GOD OF VISION AND LOVE, MAY I KEEP MY EYES
ON YOU, WAITING FOR YOU TO REVEAL TO ME NEW
POSSIBILITIES, NEW REASONS TO HOPE.

Hope in the Night

*Weeping may last through the night, but
joy comes with the morning.*

PSALM 30:5 NLT

Have you ever lain awake at two o'clock in the morning, filled with dread and despair as you think about the future? If so, you're not alone. Psychologists have found that many people are more prone to depression during the nighttime hours. This may be caused partly by our bodies' exhaustion, which affects our brains' ability to cope with negative emotions. It may also arise out of the feelings of loneliness and emptiness we often experience during the night, when we feel as though we're the only ones awake. Whatever its cause, when we find ourselves staring into the darkness, overwhelmed with anxiety, we need to remember that the sun always rises in the morning, bringing with it a new day. Even the darkest nights give way to morning's joy.

LORD, WHEN I FEEL TRAPPED BY NIGHTTIME DESPAIR, REMIND
ME THAT I'VE BEEN THERE BEFORE—AND YOU'VE NEVER
FAILED TO BRING NEW LIGHT INTO MY LIFE. EVEN WHEN I'M
BESET BY INSOMNIA AND WORRY, KEEP MY HOPE IN YOU.

God's Plans

"For I know the plans I have for you," declares
the L<small>ORD</small>, "plans to prosper you and not to harm
you, plans to give you hope and a future."

J<small>EREMIAH</small> 29:11 <small>NIV</small>

Do you ever get the feeling that God is just waiting to bop you on the head with some new problem? Your life is so full of pain that you're scared to hope for anything better; you don't want to be disappointed again. When the future seems bleak, you may be tempted to stop moving forward. If, however, you focus on God, "praying without ceasing" (1 Thessalonians 5:16), you'll find that your hope is renewed. God will bring you through those difficult seasons, and God has plans for you—plans to bless you, not to hurt you. No matter how bad things may look right now, there is hope. Nothing is impossible with God.

LORD, WHEN I'M TEMPTED TO GIVE UP, WHEN I CAN'T SEE ANY
WAY FORWARD, REMIND ME THAT YOU ALWAYS COME TO THE
RESCUE. HELP ME TO WAIT AND PRAY AND HOPE, KNOWING
THAT YOU ARE PLANNING EVEN NOW TO BLESS ME.

The Power of Love

May you experience the love of Christ, though it is too great to understand fully. Then you will be made complete with all the fullness of life and power that comes from God.

EPHESIANS 3:19 NLT

Love, whether it's given or received, empowers us. It brings new life into our hearts and minds. It allows us to see new possibilities. It gives us hope.

"God is love," the Bible tells us (1 John 4:16), and I believe we find God's presence wherever we find real love. God loves us through other people. I think He even shows us His love through our dogs and cats, those furry faithful friends of ours. But most of all, He loves us through Jesus.

The love of Christ, as the apostle Paul knew, is so vast that we will never be able to fully grasp it. But we don't have to understand Christ's love for it to change us. It is constantly working to make us strong and complete; it never stops filling our lives with the abundance of God's blessings.

THANK YOU, JESUS, FOR REVEALING GOD'S LOVE TO ME. MAY YOUR LOVE WORK IN MY LIFE AND IN MY HEART, MAKING ME STRONG, COURAGEOUS, AND FULL OF HOPE SO THAT I CAN DO YOUR WORK ON EARTH.

As Limitless as the Sky

Now all glory to God, who is able, through his mighty power at work within us, to accomplish infinitely more than we might ask or think.

EPHESIANS 3:20 NLT

No goal we set ourselves, no task we attempt, and no dream we have for the future will ever be quite as big as what God actually has in mind for us. When we focus on what we can imagine for ourselves, we may think we are envisioning our maximum potential, when actually we may be putting limits on God. The God who is all-powerful, all-knowing, and ever-present, the God of eternity and infinity, sets no boundary lines in our lives. He makes all things possible, and His creative power far exceeds our limited imaginations. He has big dreams for our lives—and God's dreams are always full of hope, power, and possibility.

INFINITE GOD, MAY I ALWAYS BE OPEN TO YOUR DREAM FOR MY LIFE. REMIND ME THAT YOU ARE AS LIMITLESS AS THE SKY. HELP ME TO TRUST YOUR POWER AT WORK IN MY LIFE. FILL ME WITH YOUR HOPE.

Forgiveness and Hope

*Peter came to him and asked, "Lord, how often should I
forgive someone who sins against me? Seven times?"
"No, not seven times," Jesus replied, "but seventy times seven!"*
MATTHEW 18:21–22 NLT

At first glance, you might think that forgiveness and hope have very little
to do with each other. A lack of forgiveness, however, can keep us tied
to the past. It can make us bitter, and it can crush our sense of hope. We
must remember that forgiveness is not forgetting or ignoring pain caused,
but it is forgiving the one who did the hurting and walking in peace and
hope for a better future.

We may feel as though forgiving someone frees that person from guilt,
but, as Jesus knew, forgiveness frees our own hearts. Refusing to forgive
locks us into the past, but forgiving makes room for new possibilities. It
gives God's Spirit space to bring divine healing into even the most painful
memories so that we can hope again.

JESUS, GIVE ME THE STRENGTH TO RELEASE THE PAST,
INCLUDING THE INDIVIDUALS WHO HAVE HURT ME.
HELP ME TO GIVE THEM TO YOU SO THAT THERE'S MORE
ROOM IN MY HEART FOR HOPE AND JOY AND LOVE.

Money

*Command those who are rich in this present world not
to be arrogant nor to put their hope in wealth, which is
so uncertain, but to put their hope in God, who richly
provides us with everything for our enjoyment.*

1 TIMOTHY 6:17 NIV

Emil Zátopek was a Czech long-distance runner best known for winning three gold medals at the 1952 Summer Olympics. When asked about his success, he did not credit it to financial backing but to hope. He said that hope in an athlete's mind was superior to money in their pockets.

The author of the letter to Timothy expressed this same insight. Notice that he doesn't say that there is anything wrong with being wealthy, but only that material riches are no reason for pride. Money is a very poor foundation for hope; instead, it can weigh us down as we run our spiritual race, and it can keep us from appreciating the joyful blessings God longs to give us.

WHEN I START TO THINK TOO MUCH ABOUT MY FINANCES,
LORD, REMIND ME THAT YOU ARE THE SOURCE OF ALL
MY JOY, ALL MY BLESSINGS, AND ALL MY HOPE.

On Eagles' Wings

Those who hope in the LORD will renew their strength.
They will soar on wings like eagles; they will run and
not grow weary, they will walk and not be faint.

ISAIAH 40:31 NIV

God doesn't want us to plod through life, resigned to the world's pain and suffering, our exhausted hearts and minds bound by earth's limitations. Instead, He wants to empower us with His love. Our faith in God is active and hopes with authority and courage, not passive and uninvolved.

When, despite our weariness, we place our hope in God, He will not only give us the power to take one more step—He will make us *fly*! We will soar on eagles' wings, and we will shine with hope.

WHEN I FEEL SO TIRED THAT I CAN'T GO ON, LORD JESUS,
REMIND ME TO LEAN ON YOUR STRENGTH. GIVE ME A HOPE
THAT BLAZES WITH YOUR LOVE AND YOUR PEACE.

Easter Hope

*What a God we have! And how fortunate we are to have him,
this Father of our Master Jesus! Because Jesus was raised from the
dead, we've been given a brand-new life and have everything to
live for, including a future in heaven—and the future starts now!*

1 PETER 1:3–4 MSG

The hope God gives us is infinite, embracing more than we can ever imagine. It includes, as Peter wrote in these verses, life that never ends, a life of wholeness and joy and infinite love that doesn't have to wait until after we die and go to heaven; it begins *now*. Easter—when Christ rose from the dead—is the full expression of the hope that is ours. We may forget what Easter really means; we lose its significance in the cultural trappings of family gatherings, Easter egg hunts, and bunnies that bring baskets stuffed with treats. But think about it: Easter is the day when Jesus triumphed over death. It's the day when we learned death doesn't have the final say in our lives. We find immense hope in Easter because of our confidence in Christ's victory over sin and death.

JESUS, THANK YOU FOR BEING BORN AS A BABY, FOR LIVING
ON THIS EARTH AS A HUMAN BEING, FOR SURRENDERING
YOUR LIFE TO THE CROSS—AND FOR RISING FROM THE
DEAD, PROVING THAT I NO LONGER HAVE TO FEAR DEATH.

A Flame in the Darkness

"Because of God's tender mercy, the morning light from heaven is about to break upon us, to give light to those who sit in darkness and in the shadow of death, and to guide us to the path of peace."

LUKE 1:78–79 NLT

If it weren't for life's dark days, we would not need hope. Death is all too real; hatred and violence are facts of life we cannot turn away from. Hope in God's mercy brings light to even the darkest nights, a light that shows us the way to a better world, a world where God's peace rules, a world where shadows are dispelled, and the Lord of love is on the throne. Hope is the voice of God's Spirit, promising us that all that was broken will one day be mended and all who are sick from sin will be healed through the power of divine grace.

MERCIFUL GOD, WHEN MY LIFE IS DARK, SHED THE LIGHT OF YOUR HOPE INTO MY HEART AND MIND. MAKE MY LIFE A FLAME THAT CARRIES YOUR HOPE OUT INTO THE WORLD SO THAT OTHERS WILL SEE THE PATH AHEAD THAT LEADS US TO YOUR PEACE, YOUR WHOLENESS, YOUR INFINITE LOVE.

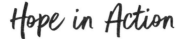

Hope in Action

Does merely talking about faith indicate that a person really has it? For instance, you come upon an old friend dressed in rags and half-starved and say, "Good morning, friend! Be clothed in Christ! Be filled with the Holy Spirit!" and walk off without providing so much as a coat or a cup of soup—where does that get you? Isn't it obvious that God-talk without God-acts is outrageous nonsense?

JAMES 2:14–17 MSG

The book of James is filled with down-to-earth insights. It's so practical that some people have struggled to understand how James' perspective can exist side by side with Paul's writings about divine grace. Martin Luther, the great Protestant reformer, was so offended by James' ideas that he called this book of the Bible an "epistle of straw" (meaning it had no lasting significance). But James never said action should *replace* grace; he only said we haven't really given God's grace control of our lives if we only talk about it and don't act upon it.

The action grace inspires is what changes our world. It brings the light of hope to the darkness of sin and sadness.

GOD, HELP ME TO TAKE ACTION SO THAT YOUR HOPE,
LOVE, AND GRACE WILL SHINE OUT INTO THE WORLD.

Nourished by Hope

You prepare a feast for me in the presence of my enemies.
PSALM 23:5 NLT

Fear is the great enemy of hope. Again and again, throughout the Bible, God says to us, "Fear not." This is the command God gives us more often than any other; in fact, some preachers say there are at least 365 Bible verses that say, "Fear not" (or words to that effect). But can we ever remove fear completely from our hearts and minds? According to psychologists, that would be an unrealistic, even unhealthy, expectation. Fear may often be our enemy, and yet it is also a normal part of human life.

But the psalmist tells us that God feeds us a feast even when our enemies are all around us. Note that the psalm doesn't say, "You destroy my enemies so that I can feast undisturbed." Instead, even when we are attacked by our old enemy fear, we can be nourished by hope.

DEAR GOD, WHEN FEAR ATTACKS MY MIND,
SHAKING MY CONFIDENCE IN BOTH MYSELF
AND YOU, MAY I FEAST ON YOUR HOPE.

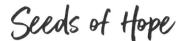

Seeds of Hope

"The Kingdom of Heaven is like a mustard seed planted in a field. It is the smallest of all seeds, but it becomes the largest of garden plants; it grows into a tree, and birds come and make nests in its branches."

MATTHEW 13:31–32 NLT

When we are discouraged, sometimes we long for some big, spectacular change to come along and turn our lives around. Often, though, that's not the way things work. Instead, we need to look for little seeds of hope in our lives—and then water them, nurture them, and wait patiently for them to grow. Today, look for little hopeful things in your life. Is the sun shining? Are the birds singing? Did something make you laugh? Did a stranger smile at you? As Jesus reminds us in the Gospel of Matthew, even the tiniest seed can grow into a tree where birds can come and nest. What "tree" might be sprouting even now in your life?

JESUS, THANK YOU FOR TELLING US STORIES THAT HELP US UNDERSTAND YOUR KINGDOM. SHOW ME SEEDS OF POSSIBILITY IN MY LIFE. SHIFT MY FOCUS AWAY FROM ALL THE BIG, DISCOURAGING THINGS IN MY LIFE SO THAT I CAN PAY ATTENTION TO THESE LITTLE SIGNS OF HOPE.

Alone Time

Before daybreak the next morning, Jesus got up and went out to an isolated place to pray.

MARK 1:35 NLT

Jesus lived a busy life, surrounded by people who were constantly clamoring for His attention and seeking His help. Sound familiar? All those people might have pushed Him back and forth until He lost His equilibrium. His disciples wanted Him to follow the crowds (Mark 1:37); the crowds wanted Him to take a political role as their king (John 6:15); and everywhere, people wanted Him to heal them (Matthew 8:16, 12:15, 15:30; Mark 6:56). Jesus knew the only way He could maintain His sense of purpose and hope was by regularly renewing His connection to His Father, and so He made the effort of spending time alone in prayer. If Jesus needed that, how much more do we! We are renewed with God's strength and energy when we spend time alone with Him in prayer. We need that energy to keep going, meeting all the demands of our busy lives. Even more, we need time alone with God to keep our hope alive.

JESUS, WHEN MY BUSY LIFE BEGINS TO DRAG ME DOWN, WHEN I FEEL MY HOPE DRAINING OUT OF ME WHILE DISCOURAGEMENT FLOODS MY HEART, REMIND ME THAT WHAT I NEED MOST IS TIME ALONE WITH YOU.

Repentance and Hope

"Produce fruit in keeping with repentance."
MATTHEW 3:8 NIV

We often think repentance has to do with guilt: examining our mistakes and expressing that we're sorry for them. In doing so, we often become discouraged and sad; we may feel shame and lose self-confidence. But this is not what God wants from us. Repentance is not about guilt so much as it is about hope. It's not wallowing in regret for the past but instead taking action to move forward. When we repent, we are filled with the hope of a future that brings us closer to Christ day by day. We gladly turn away from the things that pull us away from Him. Repentance is hope in action, leading us to a healthier, more abundant life in Christ.

CHRIST JESUS, HELP ME TO FOLLOW YOU WITH
HOPE AND ENERGY, GROWING MORE LIKE YOU AS
WE TRAVEL THROUGH LIFE TOGETHER.

Hope, Courage, and Trust

*Trust in the LORD with all your heart and lean not
on your own understanding; in all your ways submit
to him, and he will make your paths straight.*
PROVERBS 3:5–6 NIV

A lack of confidence in our own abilities can sometimes hold us back from venturing into new possibilities. We'd prefer to stick to our old familiar ruts, doing the things we know we can handle, rather than risk the embarrassment of having to learn new skills. But this is not a hopeful way to live. Hope asks that we surrender to God, fully trusting Him to lead us wherever He wants, even along unfamiliar and challenging paths. Hope, courage, and trust in God go together. They are the stepping-stones that lead us out of our ruts and into new experiences, new blessings.

LORD OF MY LIFE, MY HOPE IS IN YOU. I TRUST YOU MORE
THAN I TRUST MYSELF. LEAD ME WHEREVER YOU WANT.

Creative Hope

For we are co-workers in God's service;
you are God's field, God's building.
1 Corinthians 3:9 niv

When God created the world, He looked forward to all the beauty, fellowship, and wonder that would come. Of course, since He's God, He also knew that sin and suffering and sorrow lay ahead—but that knowledge did not keep Him from the hopeful work of creation. We are made in the image of our Creator God, and we too are called to be creators, God's fellow workers in building His kingdom. Our creativity is expressed in many ways: speaking, painting, writing, dancing, cooking, sewing, leading, teaching, inventing, healing, making music. The list goes on and on. Each act of creativity, no matter how small, is always an act of hope. When you feel your sense of hope fading away, make something! Build something! Make an active, tangible expression of hope that you and others can see.

THANK YOU, CREATOR GOD, FOR THE CREATIVE SKILLS YOU
HAVE GIVEN ME. MAY I NOT BE TOO EMBARRASSED OR SHY TO
USE THEM TO BUILD A BETTER WORLD, A WORLD OF HOPE.

Hope in the Shadows

And we know that God causes everything to work
together for the good of those who love God and
are called according to his purpose for them.

ROMANS 8:28 NLT

Sometimes, we look around at the world, and we can't help but feel anxious and afraid. When we look at our own lives, we see plenty of reasons to be discouraged and not many reasons to be hopeful. We may feel overwhelmed and exhausted; sometimes, we may even be in a state of trauma.

The Bible never denies that our world holds great pain, danger, and injustice, and following Jesus does not guarantee we won't experience hardship. Yet, no matter how dark our world is, despite the pain in our lives, love always triumphs. Somehow, God is weaving all the dismal, scary threads of our lives into a beautiful tapestry.

LORD OF MY LIFE, WHEN DISCOURAGEMENT THREATENS
TO OVERWHELM ME, REMIND ME THAT EVEN AMID MY
LIFE'S HARDSHIP, YOU ARE CREATING SOMETHING
BEAUTIFUL. RENEW MY HOPE IN YOU, I PRAY.

Joyful Expectancy

*Waiting does not diminish us, any more than waiting diminishes
a pregnant mother. We are enlarged in the waiting. We, of
course, don't see what is enlarging us. But the longer we wait,
the larger we become, and the more joyful our expectancy.*

ROMANS 8:24–25 MSG

"Joyful expectancy" is a creative way to describe hope. Like a pregnancy, hope starts out as something small, undetectable to the naked eye. But then it grows, slowly and surely, even though it is still not fully revealed. The process can't be rushed. We must surrender to its demands, nurturing the new life that is waiting to be born. Sometimes, we may feel weak and tired, overwhelmed by the immensity of what we have committed ourselves to; we may doubt our abilities to nurture this new life that is coming into the world. All we can do is be patient and trust God. Patient hope leads to new growth, new possibilities, and new revelations of God's love. These are the fruits of hope.

PATIENT LORD, ENLARGE ME WITH HOPE. EMPOWER
MY PATIENCE AND STRENGTHEN MY TRUST IN YOU.
FILL ME WITH YOUR JOYFUL EXPECTANCY.

Walking Forward

Whoever catches a glimpse of the revealed counsel
of God—the free life!—even out of the corner of
his eye, and sticks with it. . . . That person will
find delight and affirmation in the action.
JAMES 1:25 MSG

Nelson Mandela dedicated his life to dismantling racism. In the 1940s, when he was still a young man, he began fighting apartheid in South Africa, and his work continued for many decades. Imprisoned in 1964 for his activism, he was allowed only one thirty-minute visit with a single person each year and could send and receive only two letters a year. Mandela did not give up, even after twenty-seven years in prison. In 1990, he was finally released; in 1991, apartheid, at last, came to an end; and in 1994, Mandela was elected to be his nation's first Black president—and yet how easily he might have given up during his fifty-year struggle for justice! But Mandela had caught a glimpse of the "free life" to which God calls us all, and he stuck with the hard work of changing the world. He credited perseverance as the reason he didn't succumb to his circumstances. He just kept walking forward and never gave up. We too must put one foot in front of the other and persevere toward hope and promise.

FATHER, GIVE ME GLIMPSES OF YOUR PLAN FOR MY
LIFE; KEEP ME ALWAYS WALKING TOWARD YOU.

Your Best Day Ever

"Arise, Jerusalem! Let your light shine for all to see.
*For the glory of the L*ORD *rises to shine on you."*
ISAIAH 60:1 NLT

A friend of mine has a habit of saying, "Best day ever!" whenever anyone asks her how her day is going. She says it started early in her marriage when she and her husband were stumbling around getting ready for work in the morning. When she asked her husband why he was always so cheerful, even in those pre-coffee moments, he said, "Happiness is a choice!" He convinced her that she too could choose hope and happiness each morning for the day that lay ahead. And now, every single day of her life, no matter how challenging, is her "best day ever."

We too can choose to live in hope and expectancy, anticipating each morning as our "best day ever." The light of God shines on us every day, every moment.

GLORIOUS LORD, GIVE ME THE STRENGTH AND COURAGE TO CHOOSE HOPE AGAIN AND AGAIN, MORNING BY MORNING AND NIGHT BY NIGHT. MAY EACH DAY BRING ME CLOSER TO YOU.

God's Word of Power

"It is the same with my word. I send it out, and it always produces fruit. It will accomplish all I want it to, and it will prosper everywhere I send it."

ISAIAH 55:11 NLT

In Genesis, when God spoke, the world came into being—stars and planets, water and land, plants and animals, and finally, woman and man. Later in the Bible, in the Gospels, when Jesus spoke, lepers were healed (Luke 5:13), blind people recovered their sight (Luke 18:42), sins were forgiven (John 8:11), and life was restored to the dead (John 11:43). God doesn't bother with small talk. Every word He speaks is powerful. It makes things happen.

What is God speaking today in your life? It may seem like a whisper so far. You may feel that you've misheard or that it's impossible God will bring anything new into your life. But don't judge the future by the past; each day brings new hope, new possibilities, and the promise of a new blessing. Whatever God is saying to you today is just the beginning. His words are never empty.

CREATOR, SPEAK YOUR WORDS OF HEALING AND HOPE IN MY HEART AND MY LIFE. PROSPER AND BLESS YOUR WORK IN ME.

The Focal Point of Your Life

I wait for the LORD, my whole being waits,
and in his word I put my hope.

PSALM 130:5 NIV

We use the word *hope* so frivolously, so carelessly. "I hope the sun shines tomorrow," we say. Or "I hope you feel better soon." "I hope to go to Hawaii someday." "I hope I can lose weight this year." "I hope I get a raise." When the Bible talks about hope, however, it's not referring to wishful thinking, nor is it talking about any sort of ego-driven speculations about the future (such as "I hope to be rich one day" or "I hope I become a well-known musician"). Biblical hope is serious business, and it's always focused on God. It challenges us to wait patiently, even as we make up our minds to act. For the psalmist, hope was something that required the commitment of his entire being.

Hope in God isn't based on data or logic; if it were, then it wouldn't be hope! Instead, hope comes when we surrender to love and commit our entire being to trust. It springs up whenever we sharpen our focus on God.

HELP ME, LORD, TO WAIT FOR YOU, TRUST YOU,
AND PLACE ALL MY HOPE IN YOU. MAY MY ENTIRE
BEING FIND ITS FOCAL POINT IN YOU.

The Mystery of Grace

So we're not giving up. How could we! Even though
on the outside it often looks like things are falling apart
on us, on the inside, where God is making new life,
not a day goes by without his unfolding grace.

2 CORINTHIANS 4:16 MSG

"Appearances can be deceiving." It's a well-known saying, one we've probably heard repeated hundreds of times throughout our lifetimes. And yet we humans continue to judge reality by the messages we get from our five physical senses. We forget that our senses are merely portals through which we catch glimpses of God's creation; but reality is greater, deeper, and more mysterious than our senses can detect or our brains can ever fathom.

Hope is not something that depends on sight or hearing, touch or taste or smell, nor can we manufacture it by thinking hard. Instead, hope rises out from another dimension altogether. No matter what the external appearance is of our lives, the mystery of grace is always unfolding.

REMIND ME, LOVING LORD, NOT TO JUDGE YOUR PLANS FOR MY LIFE BY APPEARANCES. TEACH ME TO LIVE WITH MYSTERY. WHILE MY UNDERSTANDING IS STILL INCOMPLETE, KEEP ME ROOTED IN HOPE, ALWAYS ANTICIPATING YOUR WORK OF UNFOLDING GRACE.

Shared Hope

Let the message about Christ, in all its richness, fill your lives.
Teach and counsel each other with all the wisdom he gives.

COLOSSIANS 3:16 NLT

Hope is not something we're meant to keep private, hugging it in the secrecy of our hearts, keeping it hidden from others. Instead, it's meant to fill our lives so full that it visibly spills over where others can see it. Hope is meant to be shared.

We all have moments when our hope and faith waver, when we can't see past our pain or sadness, our frustration or anger. Despair can often seem like a dark forest in which no light or path can be found. It can feel defeating to even try to find the way out. I've been in that dark forest, and so, I suspect, have you. Sometimes, we need someone to show us the way back into the light—and other times it's our turn to be the one who says, "I've been in the place where you are standing now, but I'm not there anymore. Can I share my hope with you until you have some of your own again?"

TODAY, LORD, SHOW ME SOMEONE IN NEED OF SOME SHARED HOPE. AND THE NEXT TIME I'M FEELING HOPELESS, PLEASE SEND SOMEONE ALONG TO SHARE THEIRS WITH ME. THANK YOU THAT YOU REVEAL YOUR LOVE THROUGH US.

Quiet and Ready

*If your heart is broken, you'll find G*od *right there; if you're kicked in the gut, he'll help you catch your breath.*

PSALM 34:18 MSG

I confess, sometimes when I'm in the middle of a problem, I'm not all that interested in hope. If my heart is broken, I may be crying too loud (either figuratively or actually) to listen to what God is trying to say to me. When I'm angry about something, I sometimes want to hold on to that anger, listening to its voice instead of God's. And when I'm anxious, I often want to go over my worries again and again (and again) rather than surrender them to God.

We need to get quiet enough to hear God's voice amid our disappointing moments and be ready to act on the hope He gives. It's that "quiet and ready" piece we sometimes have a hard time with. If we can step back from our emotions, disengaging ourselves from their racket and clamor, then we can ready our hearts to once again hear the still, small voice of hope.

GRACIOUS GOD, THANK YOU THAT YOU ARE ALWAYS WITH
ME, EVEN WHEN I'M OVERWHELMED BY MY EMOTIONS.
TEACH ME TO LISTEN FOR YOUR QUIET VOICE.

God's in Control

"Do not be afraid or discouraged, for the LORD will personally go ahead of you. He will be with you; he will neither fail you nor abandon you."

DEUTERONOMY 31:8 NLT

Imagine that: God *personally* goes ahead of us in life, marking the trail so we can follow in His footsteps. This is a reality we often forget. We picture ourselves tiptoeing through the dark all alone, in danger of falling off a cliff at any moment if we take the wrong step—and meanwhile, God is right there, leading the way.

No matter how chaotic or overwhelming life seems, God sees the pattern. No matter how lost we feel, He knows the way. He never steps away for even a moment; His presence is constant, dependable, and powerful. So, there's no need to be afraid or discouraged. If we surrender our lives to God, we can live our lives with hope. He has everything under control.

LORD OF MY LIFE, WHEN I FEEL OUT OF CONTROL,
REMIND ME TO GIVE FULL CONTROL TO YOU.

The Lord Is Your Helper

*So we can say with confidence, "The LORD is my helper, so
I will have no fear. What can mere people do to me?"*
HEBREWS 13:6 NLT

We sometimes allow our lives to be controlled by fear of what other people will think. Instead of focusing on God's path of love, we wander around, pushed here and there by others' opinions of us. That's not a very hopeful way to live!

Nelson Mandela, the former president of South Africa, believed that we should be led by our hope and not by what worries us. Discriminated against, oppressed, and imprisoned, Mandela still chose to align his life with hope rather than with fear—and because he did, he brought positive change to the world. Who knows what we too can do when we rely on God as our helper! When we stop worrying about what other people think and start trusting God, hope will show us the way.

DEAR LORD, WHEN YOU CATCH ME WORRYING MORE ABOUT
OTHER PEOPLE'S OPINIONS THAN I DO YOU, DRAW MY ATTENTION
BACK TO YOU. I'M SO GLAD THAT YOU ARE MY HELPER!

Sowing Seeds

The one who sows righteousness reaps a sure reward.
PROVERBS 11:18 NIV

The Bible talks a lot about sowing seeds. This was a metaphor that made sense to communities dependent on farming for their livelihood. Today, farmers still know you can't have a harvest without first planting seeds. Those of us who make our living in other ways, though, may not have learned a farmer's patience.

Our culture often wants big results—fast! When we don't have much to show for our work yet, we may feel discouraged. Whether we're talking about professional work or spiritual, we want to have something noticeable, something impressive, to show for our effort. We haven't learned how to hope and wait for tiny seeds to sprout and grow. Be patient with yourself. Nurture the seeds of hope in your life. Wait for them to grow.

HEAVENLY FRIEND, TAKE MY IMPATIENCE FROM ME AND REPLACE IT WITH YOUR INFINITE LOVE AND HOPE.

Opportunities to Grow

*When troubles of any kind come your way, consider it an
opportunity for great joy. For you know that when your
faith is tested, your endurance has a chance to grow.*

JAMES 1:2–3 NLT

I've sometimes wondered how the people to whom James sent his letter responded to his advice about troubles. Did they sigh and roll their eyes? ("There goes Brother James again, talking nonsense.") Did they feel a little ashamed that they weren't as spiritual as good old Brother James? Or did they give it some discussion and finally start to understand what James was talking about?

Notice that James did not indicate that feeling pain is either avoidable or wrong. We're not supposed to respond to a toothache with a happy smile or give shouts of joy at a funeral. Instead, he asks us to change our *attitudes* and the way we think about trouble. Just as hard exercise makes our bodies stronger, hard experiences can make our souls stronger too. Trouble is an opportunity to grow. It teaches us how to endure, be patient, and hope.

GIVER OF LIFE, WHEN TROUBLES COME, REMIND
ME THEY ARE OPPORTUNITIES FOR YOU AND ME TO
GROW CLOSER. KEEP MY HOPE IN YOU STEADY.

Your Eternal Home

*We know that if the earthly tent we live in is
destroyed, we have a building from God, an eternal
house in heaven, not built by human hands.*

2 CORINTHIANS 5:1 NIV

When Jesus spoke about the kingdom of heaven, He always indicated that it wasn't a place far off in some spiritual realm we can only reach after death. Instead, He said His Father's kingdom was right now, right here, even right inside our hearts. At the same time, though, He promised that He would prepare an eternal home for us, a place where we will live forever with Him. This eternal home, where we live united with God, will satisfy all the unmet longings of our hearts, and it is the deepest source of our hope. By keeping in mind that we have a forever home in eternity, we can gain a better sense of perspective when we encounter trouble and tribulation in this life. If we have this perspective, even death can become a source of hope, for it will be our homegoing day.

WHEN THIS WORLD SEEMS DARK AND BLEAK, DEAR JESUS,
REMIND ME THAT MY TRUE HOMELAND IS WITH YOU IN ETERNITY.
THANK YOU FOR HAVING MY HOME READY FOR ME THERE.

Required Action

Why, my soul, are you downcast? Why so disturbed within me? Put your hope in God, for I will yet praise him, my Savior and my God.
PSALM 43:5 NIV

Even when we are at our lowest point, we always have a choice. We can choose to sink deeper and deeper into despair or we can choose to trust in God. Even when there doesn't seem to be much hope, we need but a mustard seed's worth of faith to persevere and find the hope again.

Hope and faith are similar, but they are not the same thing. Hope believes in the future; it looks forward with joyful anticipation to whatever new thing God will do next. Meanwhile, faith means to trust—and *trust* comes from the same ancient word root as *tree*: something that is firm, rooted, solid, and reliable. If we drive across a bridge, we trust it is solid enough to hold our weight. When we leap into someone's waiting arms, we trust they are strong enough to catch us; we also trust them not to turn away and let us fall. And when we trust God, we surrender the full weight of our entire lives into His care, knowing He will never fail us. In all these examples, trust is more than a belief; it requires action.

FAITHFUL ONE, ON THE DAYS WHEN I CAN FIND
NO HOPE, HELP ME STILL TO TRUST YOU.

New Paths

*"I, the Lord, have called you to demonstrate my righteousness.
I will take you by the hand and guard you, and I will give
you to my people, Israel, as a symbol of my covenant with
them. And you will be a light to guide the nations."*

Isaiah 42:6 NLT

If the choice was left up to us, our friends and loved ones would never leave us. They wouldn't move to new homes across the country, and they would live forever. The choice isn't up to us, though, and sooner or later we all find ourselves having to say goodbye to someone we love. They leave a hole in our lives when they're gone, and life may seem lonely and strange without them.

We may feel abandoned after a painful goodbye, but God is close beside us. He can use this new empty space in our lives to reveal doors we never suspected were even there, leading us out onto paths we might otherwise never have dared to follow. We may feel as though we're stumbling in the dark, but one day, we will look around and realize He has led us somewhere beautiful and bright and full of hope.

THANK YOU, FAITHFUL LORD, THAT YOU WILL NEVER
LEAVE ME. WHEN I AM FEELING LONELY AND SAD,
MISSING THE PEOPLE I LOVE, GIVE ME HOPE. HELP
ME TO BE OPEN TO A NEW PATH FOR MY LIFE.

Let God Be God!

The LORD works out everything to its proper end.
PROVERBS 16:4 NIV

Recently, sick with COVID, I worried how various church activities would survive without my contribution. I fretted over the people who depended on me in various ways, worrying that I was letting them down. I felt guilty that I couldn't do all the things I usually do to help friends and family. When I confessed to a friend how discouraged and hopeless I was feeling, she said, "Too bad the world won't run without your help. It must be hard to have the weight of all those people's lives resting only on your shoulders." I knew what she was telling me: I am not God—and He is in control of my life and all the other lives around me. It's His job to sustain and guide, not mine.

So, if you ever catch yourself feeling hopeless and anxious because, for whatever reason, you can't keep up with all the things you usually do, remember that God can. So let God be God—and rest in His arms.

I'M GLAD, LORD, THAT MY HOPE IS NOT IN MYSELF OR
MY STRENGTH. REMIND ME THAT YOU ARE WORKING OUT
EVERYTHING, EVEN ON THE DAYS WHEN I CAN'T BE MUCH HELP!

The Song of Hope

*"Very truly I tell you, unless a kernel of wheat falls
to the ground and dies, it remains only a single
seed. But if it dies, it produces many seeds."*

JOHN 12:24 NIV

Do you ever feel as though some aspect of your life has fallen into the mud and died? Maybe it's a treasured role that gave you a sense of identity (whether in your family or your profession). It might be your appearance or your physical strength. Time brings changes to our lives that aren't always welcome; in fact, they feel like losses. They may even feel like little deaths. We may wonder who we are if we can no longer do the same work or if we no longer look the same. We worry we may no longer be as important or as loved. We feel discouraged, and our sense of hope may wither.

But in the Gospel of John, Jesus reminds us that a seed must die for new life to be born—and both death and birth happen down in the dirt.

So, the next time you sorrow over the changes in your life—listen to hear the song of hope!

JESUS, WHEN I FEEL AS THOUGH A PIECE OF ME HAS FALLEN TO
THE GROUND AND DIED, REMIND ME TO WAIT AND SEE WHAT
NEW THING YOU ARE BRINGING TO LIFE IN ITS PLACE.

United in Hope

"I pray that they will all be one, just as you and I are one—as you are in me, Father, and I am in you."

JOHN 17:21 NLT

In the Bible, God often tells us that human relationships are a part of the plan to shine His hope into the world's darkness. What's more, the connections between us spread and spread: marriage partners create homes that welcome others; if they raise children, those children may carry their parents' love and hope out into the world in new shapes and forms, creating new connections; friendships attract other people, linking individuals who might otherwise never have met; and our work, our church, and our recreation give us still more opportunities to connect. We probably take it for granted, not realizing that the Spirit of God moves through all these relationships. Each friendship we forge has the potential to draw us closer to God, uniting us in His love. When the Holy Spirit brings us together, new hope grows from our unity.

SPIRIT OF LOVE, I PRAY THAT YOU WILL USE ALL MY RELATIONSHIPS TO DRAW ME CLOSER TO YOU, AND IN EACH RELATIONSHIP, MAY YOUR LOVE FLOW THROUGH ME, UNITING US IN A LIVING NETWORK OF LOVE AND HOPE.

The Power of Hope

Let's keep a firm grip on the promises that keep us going. . . . Let's see how inventive we can be in encouraging love and helping out. . .spurring each other on.

HEBREWS 10:23–25 MSG

The voyage of hope isn't a solo journey. We need each other's encouragement. The Bible tells us that we are all interconnected. My faith can encourage yours; your example of courage can inspire me. And whenever we express our sense of hope in action, we influence other lives besides our own.

We may feel we are too spiritually weak or immature to encourage others, but even a smile or a hug can make a difference in another's life. Even our tiniest acts of love may have enormous consequences, and each time we take a stand for God's justice in the world, we may set something in motion that lasts even beyond our lifetimes.

Hope is like a ripple; it starts small but grows larger moment by moment. Little by little, ripples of hope can become thundering waves of mighty power, flooding our world with the creative energy of God's love.

USE ME, I PRAY, JESUS, TO BRING HOPE TO OTHERS. MAY
YOUR LOVE FLOW THROUGH ME AND MAKE A DIFFERENCE,
NO MATTER HOW SMALL, IN THE WORLD AROUND ME.

Love

"I have loved you with an everlasting love;
I have drawn you with unfailing kindness."
JEREMIAH 31:3 NIV

God loves you. There is no better reason to be filled with hope than that! The Creator of the universe loves you now and forever. He reaches out to you each moment, His hands open to draw you closer to Him and to bless you. A love so big, so deep and wide, is hard to comprehend, especially when we realize it's not merely a generic kind of love for humanity. No, God loves *you,* the one and only individual you are, with all your quirks. He has a unique relationship with *you.*

We may never be able to grasp the fullness of God's love, even in eternity, but we can allow it to fill our lives and hearts with hope. To do that, we must stop focusing our attention on all the empty things we use to try to take the place of God's love. Let's refocus our attention on Him!

SPIRIT OF LOVE, I WANT TO TURN TOWARD YOU TODAY. I WANT TO LIVE OUT OF YOUR LOVE. I WANT TO SHARE YOUR GOOD NEWS WITH EVERYONE I SEE. MAY YOUR LOVE AND HOPE SHINE FROM MY FACE AND RING OUT IN MY WORDS. THANK YOU FOR LOVING ME.

When You're Tired and Weak

The moment we get tired in the waiting,
God's Spirit is right alongside helping us along.
ROMANS 8:26 MSG

Do you ever feel guilty for being weak? Do you feel like you're letting people down—and letting God down as well—when you're not as strong as you would like to be? You'd like to be the sort of deeply spiritual person who radiates hope and love wherever she goes, but some days you just can't manage to pull it off.

We all have those days. Days when we're tired of waiting for God's blessings to be revealed, tired of hoping when the world seems so dark . . .and just plain *tired.* That's okay. God never said He expects us to be strong all the time. When our hope falters and love seems to be in short supply, that's the moment the Spirit is right there close beside us, hands stretched out to help.

SPIRIT OF GOD, YOU KNOW MY WEAKNESS. YOU KNOW HOW EASILY I GET DISCOURAGED WHEN THINGS DON'T WORK OUT QUICKLY THE WAY I'D LIKE. WHEN I GET TIRED OF WAITING FOR YOUR PERFECT TIMING, I ASK THAT YOU INCREASE MY HOPE. WAKE IT UP, HOLD IT STEADY, LIFT IT, AND MAKE IT STRONG.

The Windows of Hope

*Open my eyes so I can see what you show
me of your miracle-wonders.*

PSALM 119:18 MSG

Troubles can keep our attention focused on our pain and suffering. Misery can make us blind to spiritual reality. Stumbling along with our heads down and our shoulders hunched, we forget to look up and see the sky. Our lives become small, dismal, and dark, and our depression grows ever deeper.

We don't have to live like that. Instead, we can turn to the one who loves us and ask Him to open our spiritual eyes. We can choose to hope when everything seems hopeless, and we can cling to God even when we can't feel His presence. And then, one day, something surprising happens: We catch a glimpse of the spiritual realm that's all around us. We look at our lives from a new perspective, and we see God's hand at work. We realize creation is filled with miracles and wonder.

LORD, OPEN WINDOWS OF HOPE SO THAT I CAN LOOK
OUT AND SEE YOUR MIRACLES AND WONDERS.

Hope vs. Despair

*That energy is God's energy, an energy deep within you, God himself
willing and working at what will give him the most pleasure.*

PHILIPPIANS 2:13 MSG

Have you ever been afraid to hope? Hoping can feel like agony sometimes because we simply don't know what will come next or when. It can seem easier to simply give up and accept the worst. Believing we can prepare for the terrible things that lie ahead gives us a small sense of control. However, most of those terrible things will never happen—and even if they do, God has a plan to shelter us and nourish us, even amid trouble.

It wasn't until recently that it occurred to me that despair is a self-focused, even arrogant, way of looking at the world. When I despair, I'm turning away from the uncertainty of hope. I'm refusing to accept that God is in control. I'm holding myself stiff and unbending rather than surrendering myself to the work of God's Spirit in my life.

HOLY SPIRIT, GIVE ME THE COURAGE I NEED TO CHOOSE TO HOPE RATHER THAN DESPAIR. I KNOW YOU ARE WORKING IN MY LIFE, AND I KNOW THAT EACH THING YOU DO COMES FROM YOUR LOVE. HELP ME TO TRUST YOU, NO MATTER HOW HARD MY LIFE SEEMS. I SURRENDER MYSELF TO YOU.

The Path of Life

*You make known to me the path of life; you will fill me with joy
in your presence, with eternal pleasures at your right hand.*

PSALM 16:11 NIV

The Bible speaks often about life as a "path" (at least fifty-six times!). The word implies that God sees our lives as journeys, with a beginning point that leads through a progression of vistas and experiences. He doesn't expect us to commit our lives to Christ and then instantly become mature saints; He knows it's a journey.

Few paths are smooth and straight; most of them have rough spots, steep stretches, and twisty curves that keep us from seeing what lies ahead. Sometimes, we wonder if we're going anywhere at all. We suspect we might even be going backward. But that's not how God sees things. Even when we feel we are lost, hopeless, and stumbling in the dark, He continues to lead. Look forward with hope. God knows where you're going even when you don't.

BELOVED PATH-FINDER, THANK YOU THAT YOU ARE
LEADING ME ALONG PATHS THAT LEAD TO YOU. WHEN THE
WAY SEEMS DARK AND FULL OF WRONG TURNS, REMIND
ME THAT YOU KNOW EXACTLY WHERE I'M GOING.

A Passion for Possibility

Jesus looked at them intently and said, "Humanly speaking,
it is impossible. But with God everything is possible."
MATTHEW 19:26 NLT

We often look at a problem and see no possible solution. An adult child's life has gotten so turned around that we don't know how to help him. Illnesses burden our family again and again, and we don't know why. An elderly parent needs help but refuses to accept it. A work situation is full of conflict and stress, but we can't afford to quit our jobs. And then there's the larger world beyond our own lives, a world where wars and pandemics and violence loom large. Problems like these can seem impossible to untangle.

But hope sees past the impossible. Hope believes in unseen possibilities. It knows that all things are possible with God. He's an expert at untangling even the most complicated problems.

GOD OF HOPE, GIVE ME A PASSION FOR POSSIBILITY. TEACH ME THAT EVEN WHEN I CAN SEE NO SOLUTION TO A PROBLEM, YOU ARE EVEN THEN PATIENTLY COMBING OUT THE TANGLES IN MY LIFE.

What's Your Name?

"I will make your name great, and you will be a blessing."
GENESIS 12:2 NIV

When the Bible speaks of making your name great, it doesn't mean you will become famous, your name recognized around the world. In the Bible, a name had to do with a person's inner identity, the very essence of who that individual was. So, what this verse is saying to you is this: "I will enlarge your identity. I will make your inner being strong." And notice that this greatness has nothing to do with ego or pride; we become bigger people not so we become arrogant and fat-headed, but so that we can bless others.

And in God's economy (unlike the world's, which is often based on "me first"), as we bless others, we too are blessed. As we encourage others, our hearts grow more hopeful. The more we help others become who they are meant to be, the more we too claim our unique identities in God.

THANK YOU, LORD, FOR GIVING ME A NAME, FOR CALLING ME TO A LARGER IDENTITY. MAY YOUR CALL FILL ME WITH HOPE, AND MAY I SHARE THAT HOPE WITH EVERYONE I ENCOUNTER.

Storytelling

Don't copy the behavior and customs of this world, but let God transform you into a new person by changing the way you think.

ROMANS 12:2 NLT

Our world has a whole range of stories it tells. Some stories emphasize courage and kindness and hope, while others focus on hatred, suffering, and despair. Some describe life as vicious and cruel, while others portray the endless possibilities of love. The narrative we believe often depends on our perspective. Even when we accept that the same facts are true, we may reach entirely different conclusions. And each story we tell about the world shapes the way we think and act.

In his letter to the Romans, the apostle Paul reminds us not to copy the world's behaviors. This means we also must be careful about accepting the world's stories. When we hold a particular narrative up to the Bible, do they match up? The Bible is always a story of hope. There's no unhappy ending, no ultimate tragedy, no cliff-hanger that leaves us wondering what comes next. The story God tells has plenty of ups and downs, but it ends with love and the eternal companionship of His presence.

STORYTELLING GOD, REMIND ME NOT TO SOAK IN THE STORIES THE WORLD TELLS ME, FOR I KNOW THEY OFTEN END WITH HOPELESSNESS AND DESPAIR. THANK YOU THAT YOUR WORD ALWAYS GIVES ME A REASON TO HOPE.

Lift Me Up, Lord

My troubles turned out all for the best—
they forced me to learn from your textbook.
PSALM 119:71 MSG

The Bible reminds us that troubles don't need to be hopeless dead ends that lead only to discouragement and failure. Instead, they are learning opportunities. They may even be occasions when our hope in God grows stronger and brighter.

As you look at your life today, what is wounding you? What troubles you? Do you see how God is using these painful situations to lift you up? If not, can you bring these circumstances to God, surrendering them to Him to do what He will? Our God is an amazing Creator, and as He works in the painful areas of our lives, His ingenuity will take us by surprise again and again. As we allow God to have His way, even seemingly hopeless problems can eventually reveal to us the wonder of God's love.

CREATOR GOD, YOU KNOW THE THINGS THAT ARE TROUBLING ME TODAY. I PLACE EACH OF THESE SITUATIONS, INCLUDING ALL THE INDIVIDUALS INVOLVED, INTO YOUR HANDS. WORK YOUR MIRACLES, I PRAY. CREATE HOPE WHERE I CAN SEE ONLY PAIN. USE THESE WOUNDS TO TEACH ME AND LIFT ME UP.

Following Jesus

*Then Jesus said to his disciples, "If any of you wants
to be my follower, you must give up your own
way, take up your cross, and follow me."*

MATTHEW 16:24 NLT

The words that Jesus spoke to His disciples some two thousand years ago still apply to us today. They give us a step-by-step formula for following Christ. The first step: give up your own way. The second step: take up your cross. Third step: follow Christ. Notice that the first step asks that we change our attitudes, shifting our focus away from the egocentric, me-first perspective most of us have always had. The second step asks us to take action, doing whatever we need to do to live out our surrender to Christ in our daily behaviors. Each person's "cross" will be something different because we all have individual circumstances with the responsibilities and opportunities that go along with them. Ultimately, though, the "cross" is always a visible, tangible expression of selfless love and hope. And finally, now that we have the right attitude and behaviors, we leave the rest up to Christ; all we must do is follow Him.

CHRIST, I WANT TO BE YOUR FOLLOWER. I GIVE MY LIFE TO YOU.
SHOW ME HOW TO EXPRESS MY COMMITMENT TO YOU IN MY DAILY
LIFE, IN ACTS OF LOVE THAT GIVE HOPE TO OTHERS. REMIND ME TO
KEEP MY EYES ON YOU SO THAT I CAN FOLLOW IN YOUR FOOTSTEPS.

Your Wildest Dreams

"No eye has seen, no ear has heard, and no mind has imagined what God has prepared for those who love him."

1 CORINTHIANS 2:9 NLT

Hope is a perspective that believes in the potential of future possibilities. That said, hope does not limit itself to what the human mind can imagine. Hope is open-ended; it doesn't insist on a certain outcome. It leaves room for surprise and wonder, as God creates things more beautiful and wonderful than anything we've ever imagined, let alone experienced.

Hope looks outward at the world around us, but it also looks inward, at our own hearts. God has amazing things in store for us. At first, we may feel uncomfortable accepting that God sees so much potential in us. It may seem arrogant or egotistical to lay claim to God's immense plans for our lives. However, this sort of hope is humble, surrendered to God. It accepts that we may never be famous or important in the world's eyes, yet we have an essential role to play in the kingdom of heaven. And we can't even imagine all that will be!

Although you can't know the future shape your life will take, God knows. It may be beyond your wildest dreams!

I AM SO GRATEFUL, GOD, FOR ALL YOU HAVE IN STORE FOR ME. WHEN YOU SEE ME TRYING TO SET LIMITS ON YOUR WORK IN ME, REMIND ME TO SURRENDER MYSELF MORE FULLY TO YOU.

The Future

There is surely a future hope for you,
and your hope will not be cut off.

PROVERBS 23:18 NIV

Mindfulness experts tell us to live in the present moment rather than the past or the future. While there is wisdom in this advice (for God does meet us in the right-now), we also cannot deny that we are creatures who live in time. Scientists aren't exactly sure what time is or if it exists outside the human mind or even if it moves at the same speed in all parts of the universe, while the Bible tells us that in eternity, time will be no more. It's nearly impossible to wrap our minds around those ideas! For now, with our limited understanding, we must settle for our concept of past, present, and future.

Hope is the Bible's word for thinking about the future. Hope believes God has good things in store for us in the days and years ahead. Hope also calls us to cooperate with God *now*, doing whatever it takes to make that future possible. Without hope, our lives would be fearful and miserable. But thanks to Jesus, we have infinite hope!

THANK YOU, JESUS, FOR BRINGING YOUR HOPE INTO OUR WORLD. MAY I ANTICIPATE MY FUTURE WITH YOU WITH JOYFUL CONFIDENCE, RESTING ON YOUR PROMISES.

God's Foolishness

For the foolishness of God is wiser than human wisdom.
1 CORINTHIANS 1:25 NIV

In a world where the rich and the powerful often seem to be the winners, while ordinary people suffer oppression and hardship, some of the Bible's promises can seem silly. "Blessed are they who mourn," for example, and "Blessed are those who are persecuted" (Matthew 5:4, 10) don't seem to make much sense. It's almost as though Jesus was looking at a completely different reality from the ordinary world we inhabit. And it's true; He *was* seeing a different world, the world of His Father's realm. But Jesus wasn't hallucinating; He wasn't crazy or delusional. He knew the kingdom of heaven was *real*. And as foolish as God's promises may sound in *this* world, in the Father's kingdom, they make perfect sense.

Anne Frank once wrote that she clung to her hopes and ideals even in the most difficult of times. If Anne Frank could cling to hope, even while she and her family were hiding from the Nazis, living in desperate fear for their lives, we can too. For it is the eyes of hope that see past this world's grim reality. It is the eyes of hope that perceive the light and splendor of God's realm.

WHEN YOUR PROMISES SEEM FOOLISH AND IMPOSSIBLE,
LORD GOD, REMIND ME TO LOOK THROUGH THE LENS YOUR
HOPE GIVES ME. TEACH ME TO SEE YOUR KINGDOM.

Even in Hard Times

That person is like a tree planted by streams of water,
which yields its fruit in season and whose leaf does not wither.

PSALM 1:3 NIV

We all have seasons in our lives when external circumstances are so bleak and cold it seems as though we're living through an ice age winter. And yet, we may discover that external conditions don't need to rob us of our inner hope.

The biblical world had different seasonal patterns than many of us experience in North America. In Bible times, people worried about times of drought rather than the bitter cold of winter. So, when the psalmist wrote that we can be like trees bearing fruit with lush green leaves despite the dry seasons that so easily stunt or destroy plant life, he was expressing that hope can keep our hearts alive and growing even during external hardship. The psalmist also knew the source of that hope. In the previous verse, he indicates that it comes from focusing our thoughts on God's teaching and instruction. When we make a habit of reading God's Word, hope flourishes in our hearts. As we ponder scripture, hope grows sturdy and tall, able to resist even the most frigid winter and the deadliest drought.

TEACH ME, LORD. WATER MY THOUGHTS WITH YOUR
WORD. SHINE THE LIGHT OF YOUR SPIRIT ON MY HEART
SO THAT MY HOPE THRIVES AND BEARS FRUIT.

The Past

*G*OD *guards you from every evil, he guards your very*
life. . . . He guards you now, he guards you always.
PSALM 121:7–8 MSG

Hope looks to the future, but a painful past can dim our vision. Sometimes, we may need to also use the lens of hope to look backward. The past need not limit our future; instead, hope allows us to see that God was with us even during trauma and suffering.

This perspective may not come easily or quickly, though. We may need the help of wise counselors and friends. Then, as we also open our hearts to the working of the Holy Spirit, we can begin to see something we may not have realized at the time: God was there with us, even in the midst of the pain, guarding us then just as He guards us now and as He will guard us in the future, all the days of our lives and into eternity.

LORD, HELP ME SEE MY PAST IN NEW WAYS, THROUGH THE
EYES OF HOPE. I KNOW YOU ARE ALWAYS WITH ME.

Rooted in Christ's Love

*Despite all these things, overwhelming victory
is ours through Christ, who loved us.*
ROMANS 8:37 NLT

Hope doesn't mean we look at the world through rose-tinted glasses, nor does it require that we live in a state of denial about the cold, hard facts of life. Instead, we know that Christ's love is the foundation of all our love.

As we learn to believe more fully in that love, trusting that Christ will never leave us or let us down, our sense of hope grows. Love is what gives us the ultimate victory. In fact, love transforms reality. In a vision, John heard Jesus say, "Look, I am making everything new!" (Revelation 21:5 NLT), and that is what He is continually doing—transforming our cold, hard realities into joyful, blooming gardens with His love.

JESUS, COME INTO MY LIFE AND MAKE IT NEW. MAY
I SEND DEEP ROOTS DOWN INTO YOUR LOVE SO THAT I
CAN GROW A HOPE THAT NEVER STOPS BLOSSOMING.

The Open Door of Forgiveness

"If you enter your place of worship and, about to make an offering, you suddenly remember a grudge a friend has against you, abandon your offering, leave immediately, go to this friend and make things right. Then and only then, come back and work things out with God."

MATTHEW 5:23–24 MSG

Sometimes we believe we can excuse our own failure to forgive. "But they hurt me too badly," we say. Or "They never said they were sorry." Or even, "I did try to express my apologies, but they refused to accept them." Jesus, however, didn't include an exception clause in His instructions. He made clear that we cannot be close to God when our relationship with another person has broken.

Forgiveness is to start fresh, to have a new beginning. This new beginning doesn't apply only to the other person. It also applies to us. A lack of forgiveness is like a closed door that prevents us from going any further, but forgiveness opens the door to new possibilities. In other words, when we forgive, we bring new hope into the world.

YOU KNOW, JESUS, HOW HARD IT IS FOR ME TO FORGIVE CERTAIN PEOPLE IN MY LIFE. TEACH ME THE WORDS TO SAY AND THE ACTIONS TO TAKE THAT WILL LEAD TO A RESTORATION OF THIS RELATIONSHIP. SHOW ME HOW TO SET HEALTHY BOUNDARIES EVEN AS I FORGIVE. BRING NEW HOPE TO THIS RELATIONSHIP, I PRAY.

Roots

"Once more a remnant of the kingdom of Judah
will take root below and bear fruit above."

2 Kings 19:29–30 niv

Our lives go through many seasons. We have fruitful seasons when it's easy to be filled with hope, as well as dry, bleak seasons when we feel as though we are withering inside and out. Changes come relentlessly into our lives: children grow up, beloved older folks leave this earth, and our bodies feel their limitations as they age, while in the larger world, trends come and go, political parties rise and fall, and triumph and despair seem to take turns having the upper hand. So, amid so much change and turmoil, how do we keep our hope steady?

Our roots in God and His love are the source of our hope, and they never change, no matter how many times the world spins around. What's more, the psalmist assures us that even while our inner root systems are spreading out in God's love, down in the soil where no one can see them, our outer lives are also growing tall and strong, bearing fruit that benefits everyone.

HEAVENLY GARDENER, NOURISH MY ROOTS WITH
YOUR LOVE SO THAT I AM FILLED WITH THE
HOPE THAT WILL ONE DAY BEAR FRUIT.

Thank You!

*Give thanks for everything to God the Father
in the name of our Lord Jesus Christ.*
EPHESIANS 5:20 NLT

"Don't forget to say thank you," we teach our children (just as our parents taught us). Too often, though, we're just being polite; we may say the words without truly feeling grateful. When Paul wrote his letter to the Ephesians, telling them to be sure to give God thanks for everything, he wasn't talking about rules of courtesy. God doesn't need us to be polite to Him. It's our own hearts that need to experience gratitude.

Gratitude shifts our attention away from ourselves and our narrow, self-centered concerns. As it affirms all that God has already done, it opens the door to hope for the future.

THANK YOU, GOD, FOR THE MANY GIFTS YOU HAVE GIVEN
ME—A HOME, FAMILY, FRIENDSHIPS, WORK, THE BEAUTY OF
THE WORLD, AND SO MANY OTHER THINGS. THANK YOU FOR
EVERYTHING. MAY MY GRATITUDE FOR ALL YOU HAVE DONE IN
THE PAST AND ARE DOING IN THE PRESENT GIVE ME JOYFUL
CONFIDENCE IN WHAT YOU WILL DO IN THE FUTURE.

Burning Bushes

*There the angel of the L*ORD *appeared to him in a blazing fire from the middle of a bush. Moses stared in amazement. Though the bush was engulfed in flames, it didn't burn up.*

EXODUS 3:2 NLT

Moses was out in the desert doing his ordinary everyday work. In his case, his job was to tend his father-in-law's sheep. In our case, our work might be sitting in front of a computer for eight hours, or it might be teaching children or caring for sick people, managing a business, or making meals for our families. Whatever our daily responsibilities are, we don't usually expect our workday to be interrupted by a vision of God's presence. We assume that if God is going to visit us in some spectacular way, it's not likely to be in the middle of our ordinary routine.

In the Bible, though, that is often how God turns up—by surprise, somewhere people aren't expecting to find Him. He startles us out of our mental ruts so we can confront a larger reality, a world that blazes with God's hope and power. When we look at the world with the eyes of hope, we too may be amazed by a "burning bush" of our own.

GOD OF HOPE AND POWER, MAY I NEVER BE SO BUSY THAT I'M NOT STARTLED TO AWARENESS BY THE FIRE OF YOUR LOVE.

A New Day

God is within her, she will not fall;
God will help her at break of day.
PSALM 46:5 NIV

We may start the day full of energy and hope but end the same day with weariness and discouragement. Sometimes the events of the day batter our hearts and minds to the point that our hope begins to ebb away. Other times, our minds and bodies are simply tired, and tired minds and bodies are more easily discouraged. Meanwhile, God never changes. He doesn't blame us for our physical and emotional reactions to a long day; instead, His love holds us steady through each day's ebb and flow. And every morning, He gives us a chance to begin again.

No matter how tired or discouraged you feel, God's Spirit never abandons you. Regardless of what happened yesterday or today, you can have hope for tomorrow because God is *within you.*

I CAN'T QUITE GRASP, GOD, WHAT IT MEANS TO HAVE
YOU LIVE WITHIN ME, BUT I BELIEVE THAT NO MATTER
HOW I FEEL PHYSICALLY AND EMOTIONALLY, YOU
ARE HOLDING ME, HELPING ME. THANK YOU FOR THE
OPPORTUNITY TO BEGIN AGAIN EACH NEW DAY.

A Good Word

Heaviness in the heart of man maketh it stoop:
but a good word maketh it glad.
PROVERBS 12:25 KJV

We all get discouraged. It's just one of those normal human emotions. We get excited about the hopes we have for the future, not realizing that we've confused "hope" with "goal setting." Then, when we realize there are obstacles in our way, and it's going to take longer than we expected to reach our goals, our hearts grow heavy, and our shoulders slump. Even people who are spiritually mature and emotionally strong go through times when they feel like giving up. "Why bother trying?" we ask ourselves. "If I'm just going to fail, why not give up?"

Times like that, we need an encouraging word from someone. And when we notice that someone else is going through a discouraging time, we can be the ones who offer encouragement and hope. Sometimes it only takes something very little—an understanding smile, a hug, or a listening ear—to renew our energy and help get us back on track.

What "good word" can you share with someone today?

SHOW ME, LORD, IF SOMEONE IN MY LIFE NEEDS
ENCOURAGEMENT TODAY, AND WHEN I'VE GOTTEN OFF
TRACK AND I FEEL LIKE GIVING UP, PLEASE SEND SOMEONE
TO LIFT MY HEART AND RESTORE MY HOPE IN YOU.

Hope for Our Enemies

"Love your enemies! Do good to them."
LUKE 6:35 NLT

Most of us are familiar with this verse. We probably wouldn't ever speak out and say we disagree with it; yet we tend to skim over it, never really absorbing what Jesus is saying to us. We believe that if someone means us harm, then we are justified in shutting them from our lives. Especially with all the talk about bullying in schools, we may even be teaching our children to hate bullies, thinking of them as enemies, undeserving of love. While our children need to learn that it's never okay for someone to abuse us, hurt us, or call us names, loving our enemies is the ultimate expression of the Golden Rule: "Do unto others as you would have them do unto you." If we want the bullies in the world to treat us kindly, then we must also show them kindness. If we love our enemies, we have the chance to turn them into friends. Loving our enemies makes room for the hope of new possibilities.

GOD, WHEN I CLAIM I DON'T HAVE ANY ENEMIES, REMIND ME OF THE PEOPLE WHO ANNOY ME, THE PEOPLE I AVOID TALKING TO, THE PEOPLE I HAVE SHUT OUT OF MY LIFE FOR ONE REASON OR ANOTHER. INSPIRE ME WITH THE HOPE THAT EVEN THE MOST BOTHERSOME RELATIONSHIPS CAN BE TRANSFORMED. HELP ME TO LOVE THE WAY YOU DO.

Memories

"Don't you see, you planned evil against me but
God used those same plans for my good."

GENESIS 50:20 MSG

Neuroscientists tell us our brains handle negative and positive memories differently. We tend to spend more time thinking about painful experiences, which means these memories may become deeply ingrained, shaping how we think about both the present and the future. Often, like hamsters circling endlessly on their wheels, we relive again and again the hurts we have received—the times we felt insulted or rejected, the times when someone made us feel small or ashamed—and in the process, we remain stuck in the past. We can't change how our brains work, nor can we change what happened in the past, but we can allow God to transform how we think about painful memories.

Ask the Spirit to reveal to you how God might use your painful memories to help you grow. Be open to exploring new possibilities that might arise from even the most hurtful experiences. Believe that God's creative power can continue to work through what has already happened to you. Let hope have the final word!

HEAVENLY FRIEND, AS I LOOK BACK AT MY PAST, SHOW ME YOUR PRESENCE AND LOVE EVEN IN THE MOST PAINFUL MOMENTS. GIVE NEW MEANING TO THESE OLD MEMORIES SO I CAN FACE THE FUTURE WITH FRESH HOPE.

The Hope of Eternal Life

God's gift is real life, eternal life, delivered by Jesus, our Master.
ROMANS 6:23 MSG

Our culture doesn't like to talk about death. Instead, we pretend that death is not an ordinary part of life. We act as though it is the ultimate tragedy—and yet it will happen to us all. A century ago, by age fifty, most people had lost many loved ones: their parents, aunts and uncles, brothers and sisters, children, and possibly a spouse. Until relatively recently, normal life contained a succession of funerals. People were born in the home and they died at home, making death both visible and familiar. These days, death is often hidden away in hospitals or nursing homes.

But no matter how we may hide it, the fear of death still haunts us. We may perceive it as a shadow lying over our lives, something terrible that robs us of hope. After all, if death awaits us all, what hope do we have? But Jesus brought a new perspective to our world. Because He conquered death on the cross, we no longer need to fear the end of this life. Instead, we can face even death with hope's joyful anticipation, trusting that God has even more wonderful things in store for us in eternity.

THANK YOU, JESUS, FOR THE HOPE I HAVE IN YOU.

Help and Hope

Stoop down and reach out to those who are oppressed.
Share their burdens, and so complete Christ's law.

GALATIANS 6:2 MSG

The Greek word translated as *law* in this verse didn't refer to something from a rule book. Instead, it had to do with the way things work, the set of rights and responsibilities that connect a community. Paul wanted the people of Galatia to understand that the community of Jesus' followers—the body of Christ—is connected by the shared responsibility of helping one another.

Recently, researchers have found that older adults who regularly spent time helping others were healthier and lived longer than those who didn't. In another study, people who gave money away had lower blood pressure than those who spent it on themselves. Yet another study found that people who regularly participated in volunteer work, helping others, experienced far fewer stress-related health conditions, such as heart disease and strokes. In other words, reaching out to those who need our help not only brings hope to others' lives; it also brings hope to our own.

LORD, SHOW ME OPPORTUNITIES TO FOLLOW
YOUR LAW OF HOPE AND LOVE.

The Hope of Glory

*God would make known what is the riches of the glory of
this mystery. . .which is Christ in you, the hope of glory.*
COLOSSIANS 1:27 KJV

In this verse, we read that Christ, the hope of glory, is within our own
small flesh-and-blood bodies. That is an amazing, immense, and almost
unbelievable statement. How can we grasp that the same Christ who was
there when the world was created, the same Christ who came to earth
some two thousand years ago, the same Christ who will reign throughout
all eternity, lives *inside of us*? The Greek word translated as *glory* meant
literally the "manifestation of God's splendor," "brilliance," and "dignity."
So, in other words, we ordinary human beings have the potential to carry
within us all that splendid light and dignity. We can be walking, talking
manifestations of hope in Christ.

Trying to wrap our minds around that is both humbling and awesome.
Christ in us is surely the greatest miracle of all. Through Him, hope takes
on new dimensions, and we capture hints of the kingdom of God in which
we truly dwell.

LORD, WHEN I LOSE MY SENSE OF SELF-WORTH, REMIND ME
THAT YOU LIVE INSIDE ME. MAY I BECOME A CLEAR LENS
TO SHINE YOUR HOPE OF GLORY OUT INTO THE WORLD.

100

The Hope of the Cross

For to be sure, he was crucified in weakness, yet he lives by God's power. Likewise, we are weak in him, yet by God's power we will live with him in our dealing with you.

2 CORINTHIANS 13:4 NIV

At the time of Jesus' death, public execution on the cross was considered a scandalous embarrassment; only lower-class criminals were usually put to death this way. For the first Christians, the cross represented something so horrific that it was hard to think about. Today, we have gone to the opposite extreme: the cross has become such a familiar symbol of Christianity that it has lost most of its power to impress. Imagine, though, if Jesus had died in an electric chair, and we then proceeded to place electric chairs at the front of every church and on top of every steeple. Picture wearing a tiny gold electric chair on a chain around your neck or on a lapel, and you may grasp a little of the horror the early Christians felt when they thought about the cross.

And yet Jesus accepted this death willingly. Jesus experienced the depths of weakness and shame so that from His death could arise new power, new life, and new hope.

THANK YOU, JESUS, FOR LOVING ME ENOUGH TO GIVE YOUR LIFE.

Humble Hope

Do nothing out of selfish ambition or vain conceit.
Rather, in humility value others above yourselves.
Philippians 2:3 niv

Our culture is not very comfortable with humility. Maybe that's because we often don't quite understand what it is. Here are a few things that humility is *not*:

- It's not letting others push us around.
- It's not being doormats who let people walk all over us.
- It's not being victims or martyrs who let others hurt us or abuse us.
- It's not being so "nice" that we avoid all conflict and confrontation.
- It's not about hiding our feelings or opinions to avoid displeasing others.

The word *humility* comes from the Latin word for earth or soil: *humus*. The humble Christ-follower doesn't have to be the most important. She doesn't interact with others from a me-first perspective. She knows who she is and that she's loved by God, so she doesn't need to put others down or be better than them to bolster her self-esteem. Humility shines out from her when she interacts with others, making them feel affirmed, appreciated, and encouraged. She brings hope to everyone she knows.

JESUS, MAY I FOLLOW YOUR MODEL OF HUMILITY.

Hope That Triumphs over Fear

"LORD, there is no one like you to help the powerless against the mighty. Help us, LORD our God, for we rely on you, and in your name we have come against this vast army. LORD, you are our God; do not let mere mortals prevail against you."

2 CHRONICLES 14:11 NIV

When we read verses like this from the Old Testament, we can claim the spiritual symbolism found in these stories of long-ago armies. We too sometimes feel powerless as we confront a situation that seems too vast for us to overcome. The Living One, the God of Israel, is also our God, and He will give us the hope and strength we need to triumph over fear. We may never face an actual army—but we too can rejoice in the victories God gives us, as He helps us conqer the difficult situations in our lives. When our hope is in God, fear never has the last word.

LIVING ONE, YOU KNOW HOW SCARED AND POWERLESS I FEEL SOMETIMES. THANK YOU THAT HOPE IN YOU GIVES ME THE STRENGTH I NEED TO KEEP TAKING TINY STEPS FORWARD. I KNOW THAT STEP BY STEP YOU ARE LEADING ME INTO THE ABUNDANT LIFE YOU HAVE PLANNED FOR ME.

Hopeful Cooperation

Two people are better off than one,
for they can help each other succeed.
ECCLESIASTES 4:9 NLT

Our world often values competition over cooperation. *Cooperation* means, literally, "to work with"—but sometimes we would rather prove we are stronger, better, faster, or smarter than the other person. In competitions, there is always one winner, while everyone else loses. Meanwhile, when people cooperate, everyone wins.

Again and again, the Bible reminds us that human relationships can be sources of hope and strength. When we offer our help and join hands with another, we are encouraged and inspired, for together we become strong enough to accomplish things we are too small and weak to do alone. Together, we climb higher and work faster. Together, we can open doors we can't open on our own. This is both a practical, physical reality and a spiritual one. When I am downhearted and hopeless, you can show me God's love and lift me up. And then, the next time you are discouraged, it will be my turn to share my hope with you.

I AM SO GRATEFUL, LORD, FOR THE RELATIONSHIPS IN MY LIFE—THE FRIENDSHIPS, THE PARTNERSHIPS, THE FAMILY MEMBERS—THAT ENCOURAGE ME AND GIVE ME HOPE. MAY I TOO BE A SOURCE OF HOPE FOR THEM.

New Life

"Look, I am making everything new!"
REVELATION 21:5 NLT

Do you ever feel as though you are old and worn out? Even if you're not actually old in years, you're so tired you feel as though you can barely keep going. When you are looking around at your life, everything looks stale, nothing is fresh; you're in a rut, and you don't know how to get out. And right about then, when you're at your weakest, disaster strikes. It could be a financial crisis, a health situation, or a family problem. Whatever it is, it just doesn't seem fair you have to go through this now!

Sometimes, though, a crisis is exactly what we need to get us out of our ruts. It's not that God is punishing us for feeling tired and hopeless; it's more like He's giving us a wake-up call so we can see what He is trying to do in our lives.

"Look," says Jesus, "I'm making everything new!"

LORD JESUS, SHOW ME THE GREEN NEW GROWTH YOU ARE
BRINGING FROM MY LIFE'S SCORCHED SOIL. MAY MY HOPE
IN YOU NEVER FALTER, EVEN WHEN I'M WEARY, EVEN WHEN
I'M IN THE MIDST OF A CRISIS. I TRUST YOUR LOVE.

In the Dark Valleys

Even though I walk through the darkest valley,
I will fear no evil, for you are with me.

PSALM 23:4 NIV

Our culture often equates darkness with evil. However, God is with us just as much in the dark as He is in the light. This means that both the dark and light experiences in our lives have things to teach us about hope. Remember, just as a baby grows in the darkness of our wombs, so do seeds sprout and grow in the darkness of the soil. Transformation and new life rise from the darkness into the light.

But it's hard to remember all that when we're walking through a "dark valley." God is still with us, but we may not be able to sense His presence. In times like that, here are some suggestions for finding glimmers of light even in the darkest valleys:

- Be grateful and express your gratitude in prayer or creative work.
- Be patient with yourself.
- Seek support from friends and family or a pastor or therapist.
- Spend more time reading scripture and in prayer.

AMID MY LIFE'S DARKEST VALLEYS, GOOD
SHEPHERD, MAY I STILL SEE STARS OF HOPE.

Taste and See

I prayed to the LORD, and he answered me. He freed me from all my fears. . . . Taste and see that the LORD is good.
PSALM 34:4, 8 NLT

David wrote this psalm before he became king, after a situation when he was so scared of his enemies that he pretended to be a drooling madman in order to escape. After his life was spared, he didn't say, "See how clever I am that I managed to get away!" Instead, he gave God all the credit.

Notice that David didn't say, "Pray and be spiritual, and then you'll experience God's goodness." Not, of course, that praying is ever wrong! But David implies that when life seems scary and hopeless, our physical senses may give us glimpses of God and renew our hope. It might be the flavor of homemade bread, the rosy light of a sunrise, or the scent of new-mown grass that brings hope to our hearts. It could be a child's laughter or a loving hug. Our favorite song, a warm bath, or even a comfy old sweater can all be opportunities to "taste and see" God. And through each of these small sensual pleasures, God whispers hope into our hearts.

TODAY, LORD, OPEN MY EYES TO THE BEAUTY OF YOUR WORLD. REMIND ME TO TAKE A MOMENT TO LISTEN, SMELL, TASTE, AND FEEL ALL THE WONDERFUL THINGS YOU HAVE CREATED. MAY I TASTE AND SEE YOU AND FIND NEW HOPE.

Thoughts

For as he thinketh in his heart, so is he.
PROVERBS 23:7 KJV

Psychologists tell us that our thoughts shape our lives. Neurological research even suggests that our brains connect negative thoughts and memories in ways that can rob us of hope. For example, a colleague at work says a cross word to you, and you find yourself feeling discouraged about your weight. You get in a fight with your husband, and for the rest of the day, you worry you might lose your job. These things have nothing to do with each other in reality, but if we allow ourselves to dwell on our hurt feelings and discouragement, they can create a spreading network of brain-cell connections that are easily triggered every time we encounter even the most trivial negative situation.

Fortunately, the opposite is also true: we can create positive thought habits that will empower our faith and fill our lives with hope. Beginning every day with gratitude fills our hearts and minds with the hope that we find in Jesus.

YOU KNOW, LORD, HOW EASILY I CAN SINK INTO NEGATIVE THOUGHTS. I NEED YOUR HELP WITH THIS. TEACH ME TO REPLACE THOSE SELF-DEFEATING, HOPE-ROBBING THOUGHTS BY MEDITATING ON YOU AND THE MANY BLESSINGS YOU HAVE GIVEN ME.

The Truth

"If you stick with this, living out what I tell you, you are my disciples for sure. Then you will experience for yourselves the truth, and the truth will free you."

JOHN 8:31–32 MSG

The truth Jesus is talking about in this verse is the message He came to bring us from the Father: God loves us, and through Jesus, we have hope not only for this life but for all eternity. This is a truth that can't just be believed with our minds alone; it needs to be experienced, "lived out," as Jesus says here.

In other words, experiencing truth for ourselves is often a process. Although some of us (the apostle Paul, for example) have amazing, instantaneous conversions, even then we need time for the truth to do its work in us. Paul, after his experience on the road to Damascus, did not instantly begin his ministry for Christ; he needed to spend three years in the desert, allowing the truth of Christ to do its work, experiencing it for himself. This is a process we must each go through discovering for ourselves that Christ's truth has set us free to hope, even amid the world's darkness and despair.

JESUS, I WANT TO FOLLOW YOU. MAY YOUR
TRUTH SET ME FREE TO HOPE.

Paths of Hope

Speak encouraging words to one another. Build up hope so you'll all be together in this, no one left out, no one left behind.

1 THESSALONIANS 5:11 MSG

The word *encouragement* comes from older words that meant "put courage into." When we speak encouraging words, as Paul recommends in this verse, we are doing more than simply complimenting someone or building up their self-esteem. Our words have the power to strengthen each other's hearts, to give each other hope.

Parakaleó, which is the Greek word used in this verse, had to do with walking close beside someone, teaching them, strengthening them, and comforting them. A similar word—*Paraclete*—refers to the Holy Spirit, who is the divine encourager, our companion and helper throughout life. Here, once again, we see that God uses relationships to build His kingdom. As we make our spiritual journeys, mutually helping each other, together we create paths of hope for others to also see and follow.

JESUS, MAY I ENCOURAGE OTHERS, EVEN AS THEY ENCOURAGE ME. MAY WE WORK TOGETHER TO BUILD PATHS OF HOPE THAT LEAD US—AND OTHERS TOO—INTO YOUR PRESENCE.

The New Creation

Therefore, if anyone is in Christ, the new creation
has come: The old has gone, the new is here!

2 CORINTHIANS 5:17 NIV

Following Christ doesn't mean we won't still experience the world's pain and suffering. At the same time, however, we don't have to wait until after we die to experience the new creation of Christ. It's almost like we live in two dimensions at once—and Christ's dimension is in the process of transforming the world's dimension. It is our hope and faith in Christ's transformative power that is what changes the world around us and creates a ripple effect. This is a perspective we need to grasp and experience for ourselves. When we do, it will give hope to even the most difficult days.

CHRIST JESUS, HELP ME TO REMEMBER TODAY THAT I
LIVE IN YOUR DIMENSION AS WELL AS THE WORLD'S
DIMENSION. GIVE ME GLIMPSES OF YOUR NEW CREATION
SO THAT I CAN LIVE MY LIFE WITH GREATER HOPE.

Steps to Forgiveness

*Be kind and compassionate to one another, forgiving
each other, just as in Christ God forgave you.*
EPHESIANS 4:32 NIV

When we forgive others, we bring new hope to both their lives and ours. This isn't only true in the spiritual realm; researchers have found that forgiving others is good for our bodies as well. Sometimes, though, we've been hurt so badly that forgiving seems impossible. If that's the case, here are some steps we can take to help us forgive:

- Face the painful memories. Psychologists say that avoiding the hurt can allow it to become like a piece of petrified wood that never changes. Facing those old memories doesn't mean wallowing in them; it means allowing ourselves to process them and work through them with the Holy Spirit's help (and sometimes with the help of a friend, counselor, or pastor).

- Put yourself in the shoes of the person who hurt you. Try to understand what motivated their actions and allow yourself to feel their pain.

- Make a *choice* to forgive. Ask for God's help, regardless of your emotions.

HOLY SPIRIT, HELP ME TO FORGIVE, BRINGING NEW
HOPE TO OTHERS' LIVES AS WELL AS MY OWN.

Nature's Message

The heavens proclaim the glory of God. The skies display his craftsmanship. Day after day they continue to speak; night after night they make him known. They speak without a sound or word; their voice is never heard. Yet their message has gone throughout the earth, and their words to all the world.

PSALM 19:1–4 NLT

The ancient Christian Celts referred to nature as the "second Book of God." They meant that while scripture is God's Word, nature too reveals God's glory—and we do well to take the time to "read" what God is saying in the natural world. We can find powerful spiritual messages there, both in nature's beauty and in its rhythms and cycles.

Again and again, the Bible speaks of God revealing Himself to people when they are "in the wilderness"—in other words, outside in the natural world. Jesus Himself sought out times alone in nature, retreating to those quiet secluded places to restore His connection with His Father (see Matthew 14:13, John 6:15, Mark 1:35, Luke 6:12).

So, the next time you're feeling discouraged with life, try spending some time alone outside. The world of nature can renew your hope in God.

CREATOR GOD, MAY I NEVER BE TOO BUSY TO NOTICE YOU SPEAKING TO ME THROUGH A SUNRISE, BIRDSONG, OR THE WIND IN THE TREES.

Conversations of Hope

"For where two or three gather in my name, there am I with them."
MATTHEW 18:20 NIV

When Jesus spoke these words, He wasn't saying that there's something magical about a gathering of just any two or three people. Instead, He was referring to the way His Spirit lives in relationships. Friendship can help us in our spiritual lives. And yet in friendship, as in other parts of our spiritual lives, we often "fall asleep": we take a friend for granted, forgetting that friendship, like all relationships, requires steady effort and faithfulness. We need to not only share ourselves in friendship but also be willing to listen deeply. These are the kinds of conversations that allow us to bring to light truths that each of us alone would never have discovered. They encourage us and strengthen us and bring new hope into our lives. This is the perspective on friendship that makes room for the presence of Christ.

THANK YOU FOR MY FRIENDS, JESUS. MAY I REMEMBER THAT FRIENDSHIP IS ABOUT GIVING AS MUCH AS IT IS RECEIVING. MAY MY FRIENDS AND I EXPERIENCE YOUR PRESENCE IN OUR RELATIONSHIP, AND MAY WE GUARD EACH OTHER'S HOPE.

Buried with Christ

We were therefore buried with him through baptism into death in order that, just as Christ was raised from the dead through the glory of the Father, we too may live a new life.

ROMANS 6:4 NIV

When we think of the temptation to sin, we often have in mind the attraction we may feel to illicit and harmful behaviors. If we're not experiencing those attractions ourselves or we find it easy to resist them, then we may think we don't have a problem with temptation. We assume that when it comes to the enemy of our souls, we're doing just fine. Yet, we would do well to remember that temptation can be more subtle. The enemy can tempt us into believing we aren't doing enough for the kingdom, which causes us to quit trying. Or we are tempted to think we are doing just fine on our own and don't need Jesus' redemptive work on the cross.

Christ doesn't want His followers to plod through life with sad and tired faces. That old way of living needs to die and be buried so that Christ can make our lives fresh and new and filled with resurrection hope.

CHRIST, I THANK YOU THAT MY OLD LIFE OF DISCOURAGEMENT AND DESPAIR IS BURIED WITH YOU. HELP ME TODAY TO EXPERIENCE THE HOPE AND ENERGY OF YOUR NEW LIFE.

The Hope of Following Jesus

Jesus looked around and saw them following. "What do you want?" he asked them. They replied, "Rabbi" (which means "Teacher"), "where are you staying?" "Come and see," he said.

JOHN 1:38–39 NLT

Before you can get anywhere in life, you first must make the decision to not stay where you are. This, in effect, is the message Jesus is giving to us in this story from the Gospel of John. If we want to experience the hope and joy of following Christ, then we have to decide to leave our old lives behind—and then we must follow Jesus and see where He lives. Yet again, Jesus tells us that following Him is something that requires action on our part. Yes, the first step is to make up our minds that we want to leave our old lives so that we can experience the new life of Jesus, but then we must put that decision into action. We have to change the way we live. This means seeing for ourselves where and how Jesus lives and then imitating His pattern of life, making it real in our ordinary daily lives. Then, as we see Jesus more and more clearly, our lives will be made new, filled up with love, joy, and hope.

JESUS, I WANT TO FOLLOW YOU. I WANT TO SEE WHERE AND HOW YOU LIVE. I WANT TO BE LIKE YOU.

Let There Be Light!

God said, "Light up the darkness!" and our lives
filled up with light as we saw and understood God
in the face of Christ, all bright and beautiful.
2 CORINTHIANS 4:6 MSG

In the book of Genesis, God says, "Let there be light!"—and light shines out. Today, in our own lives, God continues to call forth light. That light is not for our lives alone; like the moon that reflects sunlight into the night, we too are called to shine with the hope of Christ. We do this by

- demonstrating to others that while we still see the darkness, we don't let it keep us from also seeing the hope and beauty in the world;

- reaching out to help others in tangible and practical ways;

- shielding our light from the world's tempests so that it burns steadily, even during the times when we are experiencing troubles of our own;

- allowing people to see that it's Christ living in us who allows us to remain hopeful, even in the face of challenges and hardship;

- doing whatever we can to help others see more clearly.

None of these mean we shove our beliefs down other people's throats. We simply live out the love and light that Jesus has given to us.

LET ME SHINE, DEAR JESUS, WITH YOUR LIGHT.

The Anchor of Your Soul

We who have fled to take hold of the hope set before us may be greatly encouraged. We have this hope as an anchor for the soul, firm and secure.
HEBREWS 6:18–19 NIV

Hoping for things that can't possibly happen is not the sort of hope the Bible describes. We don't hope that we'll grow bird's wings. . .or that our husbands will wake up one day as perfect individuals who will never frustrate us again. . .or that our children will never get muddy or tear their clothes. The Bible's hope accepts the real world with all its limitations. It doesn't have anything to do with fantasy or make-believe. Instead, it's something real and solid. Although we don't know the exact shape and size of everything God has in store for us, we are anchored in the confidence that our futures are held steady in His love.

LORD, MAY MY HOPE IN YOU HOLD MY LIFE STEADY EVEN IN THE WILDEST STORMS. BE MY ANCHOR, I PRAY, TODAY AND EVERY DAY.

Planting in Tears

Those who plant in tears will harvest with shouts of joy.
PSALM 126:5 NLT

Notice that this verse doesn't say, "Those who retreat from life and sit sobbing endlessly in their bedrooms will harvest with joyful shouts." Instead, the psalmist acknowledges that sometimes we can't help crying—but at the same time, we are called to continue the active work of carrying Christ's hope out into the world. This is the sort of hope psychologists tell us makes optimism so practical; optimism is not mere wishful thinking but rather the belief that our actions can make a difference in the world.

Your tears may water the seeds you plant today, but remember the joyful harvest that lies ahead.

GIVE ME THE STRENGTH I NEED, FAITHFUL LORD, TO
CONTINUE PLANTING SEEDS OF HOPE EVEN WHEN MY
OWN HEART IS BREAKING, AND I'LL TRUST THAT ONE
DAY, THOSE TINY, NEARLY INVISIBLE SEEDS WILL GROW
INTO HEARTY, FRUIT-BEARING PLANTS OF LOVE.

Hope for New Paths

"The LORD will guide you continually, giving you water when you are dry and restoring your strength. You will be like a well-watered garden, like an ever-flowing spring."

ISAIAH 58:11 NLT

Hope is not a passive emotion that allows us to curl up and be lazy. Instead, hope pushes us forward onto unexplored paths. It is the voice of God guiding us into new adventures, encouraging us to try new things, grow, and be bold in ways we've never been before. This doesn't mean there won't be times when we need to take some time out to rest; constant busyness is not what hope in God looks like either. Instead, this hope that is ours relies on God's daily and ongoing sustenance. When our hearts are dry, He waters them. When we feel weak, He restores our strength. When we lack courage, His love nourishes our fearful hearts.

Hope isn't about ego or do-it-yourself self-reliance. We cannot manufacture it on our own or take off running with it in a solo race. Hope depends on God because our hope springs from God.

GUIDE ME, LORD. GIVE ME COURAGE, AND WATER MY HEART WITH YOUR LOVE. GIVE ME THE ENERGY I NEED TO VENTURE OUT OF MY RUTS INTO YOUR PLAN FOR MY LIFE. ALL MY HOPE IS IN YOU.

Give It to God!

*Commit to the LORD whatever you do,
and he will establish your plans.*

PROVERBS 16:3 NIV

Sometimes when we look at our lives, we see more failure than successes, more endings than beginnings. No one likes to fail; not only are we disappointed that something we cared about did not come to fruition, but our self-esteem may also suffer. We may feel embarrassed or ashamed, especially if we think the failure was our fault. Proverbs' wise author, however, encourages us to look at our lives from a different perspective. When we commit all our efforts to God, then we can let go of our need for success.

We do not know what plan God has for our lives and the world. What to us looks like failure may be the beginning of something new and wonderful. When we depend on God to uphold everything we do, we leave the results in His hands.

ALL-KNOWING GOD, GIVE ME HOPE WHEN FAILURE
AND ENDINGS ARE WEIGHING HEAVILY ON MY MIND.
REMIND ME TO GIVE EACH SITUATION TO YOU.

Shepherd of Hope

*"GOD, the Master, says: From now on, I myself am the shepherd.
I'm going looking for them. As shepherds go after their flocks
when they get scattered, I'm going after my sheep. I'll rescue them
from all the places they've been scattered to in the storms."*
EZEKIEL 34:11–12 MSG

Sometimes, we're hard on ourselves. We realize we've taken a wrong turn in life, and we beat ourselves up for it. We can get so mired in guilt and regret that we feel stuck, hopeless, and unable to see a way forward. But the Bible assures us that God is with us even in our mistakes.

If you've lost your way and you find yourself somewhere dark and scary, God doesn't want to punish you, nor does He want you to punish yourself. Instead, He's waiting patiently to rescue you and lead you back onto His path of abundant life. You can never get to the point where your life is hopeless. Even now, no matter what you've done or how impossible circumstances seem, the Good Shepherd is looking for ways to guide you home.

SHEPHERD OF MY SOUL, THANK YOU THAT I CAN NEVER GO BEYOND
YOUR LOVE. I KNOW THAT WHEN MY LIFE SEEMS HOPELESS, YOU
ARE STILL MY HOPE. THANK YOU THAT YOU ALWAYS RESCUE ME.

The Kingdom of God

"The kingdom of God is in your midst."
LUKE 17:21 NIV

Sometimes, Christ's followers forget that God's kingdom is right here, right now, all around us. Since we will one day know the joy of eternity, Christians may act as though we have no responsibility for this world. They talk about how terrible the world is, as though there's no hope for it; sin and rebellion against God are all around, so we might as well forget about trying to make the world a better place. When Christians focus only on the hereafter, it can lead to indifference to our world's critical problems. Why bother taking care of our planet since God is preparing for us a new earth? Why worry about poverty and sickness when God will wipe away all tears in heaven? But Jesus never had that attitude. He did whatever He could to help everyone He encountered, demonstrating His love by mending crippled legs, restoring sight, healing diseases, feeding the hungry, and seeking out the lonely and forgotten.

Jesus calls us to stop living in the dreary districts of hopelessness and step into His kingdom of active hope, energetic joy, and tangible love.

PULL ME OUT OF THE HOPELESS REGIONS THAT
HAVE GROWN SO FAMILIAR, LORD, AND TEACH ME
TO LIVE MY LIFE IN YOUR KINGDOM, EMPOWERED
BY YOUR SPIRIT TO BUILD A WORLD OF HOPE.

Deceptive Emotions

Keep a firm grip on the faith. The suffering won't last forever.
It won't be long before this generous God who has great plans for us
in Christ—eternal and glorious plans they are!—will have you put
together and on your feet for good. He gets the last word; yes, he does.
1 PETER 5:10–11 MSG

Despite what our emotions sometimes tell us, the hope of Christ always has the last word. No matter how sad and discouraged we feel, those are only feelings; they say nothing about spiritual reality. Yes, human life is filled with physical, emotional, and spiritual pain—there's no denying that—but even amid suffering, we can cling to the hope we have in Jesus. Even when our prayers seem to go unanswered, and we see no evidence that God is in control of the events in our lives, even then we can continue to hope. Our hope is built on trusting God.

TEACH ME, JESUS, TO RELY MORE ON YOU THAN I DO MY
EMOTIONS. REMIND ME THAT MY FEELINGS CAN DECEIVE ME.
THEY CAN CLOUD MY PERCEPTION OF SPIRITUAL REALITY.
KEEP MY HOPE ALIVE AS I TRUST MY LIFE TO YOU.

Hold On!

"This vision-message is a witness pointing to what's coming. . . . And it doesn't lie. If it seems slow in coming, wait. It's on its way. It will come right on time."

HABAKKUK 2:3 MSG

The book of Habakkuk was written nearly three thousand years ago, and yet human nature hasn't changed. The prophet Habakkuk understood how easy it is to have our hope overcome by doubt and impatience. We look around us, and we can't help but wonder if our hope in God is nothing but a lie. In this verse, Habakkuk reassures us that God never lies, and He knows exactly what He's doing even when we don't.

God understands your impatience and doubt. But He asks you to hold on a little longer. Wait and see the amazing things He is doing even now.

WHEN MY HOPE FADES, LORD, AND ALL I CAN FEEL IS FEAR AND DOUBT, GIVE ME THE PATIENCE I NEED TO WAIT FOR YOU.

Your Whole Self

Let all that I am wait quietly before God, for my hope is in him.
PSALM 62:5 NLT

Imagine if you were driving down the road at sixty miles an hour, and you decided to drag one foot on the ground while the rest of you remained in the car. That one little piece of you that wasn't inside the car would have disastrous, possibly even fatal, effects. David, the probable author of this psalm, emphasizes that we need to wait for God with *all* our being. It's easy, though, to sometimes feel fragmented. When we encounter a problem in our lives, part of us may believe that God is still in control, but at the same time, another part of us doubts and wonders if the situation might be hopeless.

Regardless of our emotional reactions, though (for sadness and fear are normal human responses), we can commit our entire lives, every piece of our beings, to God. Even when problems threaten to overwhelm us, we can continue to commit everything to God, waiting for His face to be revealed to us.

LORD, I WANT TO GIVE YOU MY WHOLE SELF, EVERY BIT OF ME. SHOW ME IF I AM HOLDING ANYTHING BACK. KEEP ME HOPING, WAITING FOR YOU TO SHOW ME YOURSELF.

God Won't Let You Drop!

"God is not a man, so he does not lie. He is not human, so he does not change his mind. Has he ever spoken and failed to act? Has he ever promised and not carried it through?"

NUMBERS 23:19 NLT

Have you ever done the team-building exercise that's referred to as a *trust fall*? It requires that you deliberately drop backward, blindly trusting that the person behind you will catch you. Most people have trouble doing it the first time, but it gets easier with practice. Each time we fall backward and are caught, our trust builds.

Sometimes, life feels a lot like a trust fall. We can't see God, and yet He asks us to drop our whole life into His hands. The first time we truly lean our entire weight on Him, it can feel scary. What if He's not there? What if He drops us? That that will never happen! God's arms are strong, and we can be confident that He loves us too much to ever let us fall. Our hope in God isn't a wish. Even during the times when we have no sense of His presence, He will never, ever let us fall.

THANK YOU, GOD, THAT YOU ALWAYS CATCH ME. YOU WILL NEVER DROP ME. MY HOPE IS IN YOU, AND I KNOW I CAN TRUST YOU.

Don't Limit God!

GOD *doesn't come and go. God lasts. He's Creator of all you can see or imagine. He doesn't get tired out, doesn't pause to catch his breath.*
ISAIAH 40:28 MSG

Human beings shape their expectations by what they have already experienced. We generalize things that may be true, but because our experiences are limited, sometimes our expectations may be false. For example, we've seen the sun rise every day of our lives, so we expect it to rise again tomorrow—and that expectation is justified. But suppose we've been bitten more than once by a dog; are we then correct to assume all dogs are dangerous? Or if we've been betrayed by more than one friend, should we believe that no friendship can be trusted?

We do the same thing with God. Based on our experience with human beings, we find ourselves expecting God to inevitably, sooner or later, let us down. We can't believe He could be loving enough or strong enough to meet all our hopes. Yet God is not like human beings. He never gets tired, He never gives up, and His love has no end.

WHEN I PLACE LIMITS ON MY HOPE IN YOU, LORD, REMIND ME THAT YOUR LOVE AND POWER EXCEED ANYTHING I HAVE EVER EXPERIENCED, ANYTHING I CAN EVEN IMAGINE.

A New Song

He put a new song in my mouth, a hymn of praise to our God.
PSALM 40:3 NIV

When life seems hopeless, sometimes the best thing we can do to restore our sense of hope is to sing. From a physical standpoint, research has found that singing benefits our nervous systems by helping to reduce stress. One study found that people who sing regularly either improve or maintain good mental health. Singing also encourages us to breathe more deeply, which can heighten our sense of well-being. From a spiritual perspective, the Bible often speaks of the power of song to express praise, lift our spirits, and give us a greater sense of God's presence. So, the next time you find your hope wavering—sing!

LORD JESUS, WHEN I BEGIN TO LOSE HOPE, WHEN I
SEE NO REASON WHATSOEVER TO SING, REMIND ME
THAT YOU YOURSELF ARE MY SONG. EVEN IF I CAN'T
CARRY A TUNE, MAKE YOUR MUSIC IN MY LIFE.

A World of Righteousness

We are looking forward to the new heavens and new earth
he has promised, a world filled with God's righteousness.

2 PETER 3:13 NLT

God wants us to be actively engaged in this world, with all its problems and challenges. But as we work to build God's kingdom here on earth, we will be encouraged if we balance our outlook with the awareness that, ultimately, God will create a new world that overflows with His goodness and love. This perspective can keep us hopeful, even when everything around us insists that there cannot possibly be any hope. With the assurance of that hope firmly grasped, we will have more strength to do the work that God calls us to in this life.

GOD OF GOODNESS, I LOOK FORWARD WITH JOYFUL
ANTICIPATION TO SHARING WITH YOU A NEW WORLD
WHERE NOTHING IS BROKEN, WHERE ALL ARE HEALED,
WHERE LOVE REIGNS AND HATRED IS BANISHED.

Mystery

My goal is that they may be encouraged in heart and united in love,
so that they may have the full riches of complete understanding, in
order that they may know the mystery of God, namely, Christ.

COLOSSIANS 2:2 NIV

In the Bible, the word *mystery* doesn't refer to a whodunit or a puzzle to be solved. Neither is it something that is completely unknowable. Instead, it indicates something very real that exists outside the box of our previous experience. It's something we can only perceive as God reveals it to us, and when He does, it stretches our understanding and widens our perspective. This verse from the book of Colossians tells us that Christ Himself is the revelation of the divine mystery. Although we still cannot understand all that God is, when we look at Christ, we see the embodiment of God, the full expression of His love, and the ultimate assurance of all our hope.

As we continue to follow Christ, getting to know Him better and better, both our hope and our understanding will grow stronger, wider, and brighter.

THERE IS SO MUCH ABOUT YOU THAT I STILL FIND MYSTERIOUS.
LORD GOD. THANK YOU THAT THE WONDER OF YOU NOT ONLY
GIVES ME HOPE BUT ALSO STRETCHES MY ASSUMPTIONS TO
MAKE MORE ROOM FOR YOUR SPIRIT IN MY HEART AND LIFE.

Light

"The people living in darkness have seen a great light; on those living in the land of the shadow of death a light has dawned."

MATTHEW 4:16 NIV

Imagine you are standing in a shadow that stretches around you in every direction. In the darkness, you can't make out the shape of your surroundings. You can't see anyone, so you assume you are alone. You feel lost, afraid to take a step in any direction, and paralyzed by hopelessness and anxiety. You ask yourself, *What if I'm stuck here alone forever?* Your anxiety grows stronger as you become certain there is no way out of this shadowland.

And then suddenly, a strong wind blows away the clouds. The sun blazes down on you from a blue sky. You blink, and once your eyes adjust to the light, you look around only to discover that the person you love best in all the world is there beside you. He smiles and takes your hand, and together you explore the beautiful land of green hills and valleys that were there all along.

Nothing changed in this scenario except for the presence of light—and in our lives, the light of God makes all the difference.

SHINE YOUR LIGHT ON ME, LORD, AND GIVE ME HOPE.

Glimpses

I consider that our present sufferings are not worth comparing with the glory that will be revealed in us.

ROMANS 8:18 NIV

Today, amid whatever suffering you are experiencing (whether it's trivial or immense, physical or emotional, chronic or fleeting), ask God to give you a "peephole" to peek through, a tiny glimpse of the glory and splendor that He has in store for you.

And notice that in this letter to the Romans, Paul indicates that this glory will be revealed *in us*. God intends that each one of us, despite all our flaws and failures, our heartaches and physical limitations, will become shining beacons of hope.

GOD, IT'S HARD FOR ME TO BELIEVE THAT I WILL EVER SHINE WITH GLORY; BUT MY HOPE IS YOU, NOT MYSELF OR MY OWN ABILITIES. WHEN I FEEL MOST DISCOURAGED WITH MYSELF, PLEASE GIVE ME JUST A GLIMPSE OF THE PERSON YOU INTEND ME TO BE.

Expectation vs. Hope

You can make many plans, but the LORD's purpose will prevail.
PROVERBS 19:21 NLT

Our expectations are not the same as hope. We might expect that the sun will shine tomorrow, only to have the clouds pour down rain from sunrise to sunset. At work, we may expect to get a substantial raise that never materializes. We may expect to impress people with our talent, only to find them uninterested in our abilities. Expectation makes plans. It believes it's in control and has the future all figured out. It thinks it knows exactly what tomorrow will look like. Meanwhile, hope realizes that it doesn't know what the future will be, but it *does* know that the future is in God's hands. It is confident that no matter what happens, God's purposes are prevailing.

REMIND ME, LORD, THAT EXPECTATION AND HOPE ARE NOT THE SAME THINGS. WHEN I TRY TO TAKE CONTROL OF THE FUTURE WITH PLANS AND EXPECTATIONS, REMIND ME THAT YOU KNOW BETTER THAN I DO AND I CAN TRUST YOUR LOVE.

Hopeful Choices

The righteous choose their friends carefully,
but the way of the wicked leads them astray.

PROVERBS 12:26 NIV

There are things we can do to make a positive difference in our outlooks and actions we can take that will increase our sense of hope. One of these things is choosing with whom we spend time. The right kind of friends will encourage us rather than drain our hope and energy.

We can also be careful about what we read and watch. If we continually stuff our minds full of doom and gloom, we may find our hope ebbing away. We can choose instead to read books and watch programs that renew our hope. This doesn't mean our friends always have to be cheery and good-natured, that every book we read must have a happy ending, or that every television program we watch is a Hallmark Special. But when we leave a friend, finish reading a book, or turn off the television, our hope should be intact rather than swamped with despair or doubt. The choice is ours to make.

HELP ME, LORD GOD, TO CHOOSE MY FRIENDS WISELY. REMIND
ME TO BE DISCRIMINATING WHEN IT COMES TO WHAT I
READ AND WATCH. SHOW ME HOW TO NURTURE MY HOPE
IN YOU RATHER THAN ALLOWING IT TO BE WEAKENED.

Love Is What Matters

Prophecy and speaking in unknown languages and special knowledge will become useless. But love will last forever!
1 CORINTHIANS 13:8 NLT

Sometimes we pride ourselves on our skills, talents, and achievements. On the other hand, we doubt ourselves if we feel we are not good enough to excel at anything. If we look at our lives and realize we've made no major contribution to the world (at least from our own perspectives), our self-esteem may falter.

Meanwhile, the Bible tells us that God is not as impressed by fame or fortune as He is by our ability to love. If we did nothing in life except allow His love to flow through us in countless tiny ways, blessing the lives of others, God would consider us to be successes. God gives us many abilities with which to serve Him, but it's love that truly lasts on into eternity.

REMIND ME, GOD, THAT LOVE IS MY HIGHEST GOAL. EVEN IF THE WORLD NEVER SEES ME AS SUCCESSFUL, MAY I ALWAYS BE A VEHICLE OF YOUR LOVE, BRINGING HOPE TO EVERY PERSON I MEET.

Encourage the Stragglers and the Strugglers

Gently encourage the stragglers, and reach out for the exhausted, pulling them to their feet. Be patient with each person, attentive to individual needs. . . . Look for the best in each other, and always do your best to bring it out.

1 Thessalonians 5:14–15 msg

If we see someone struggling in life (perhaps battling an addiction, sinking into despair, or overflowing with anger), our first impulse should not be to judge or condemn; instead, God asks that we reach out our hands to help and encourage. If you have a friend who loves to gossip, instead of complaining about her to other friends (which is itself gossip!), focus on what is good in her and do your best to strengthen that in her. Instead of always yelling at your children for their mistakes, catch them succeeding and let them know you noticed. Comment on your husband's strengths rather than constantly criticizing his failures. As we shift our attention to lifting others rather than dragging them down, the hope and love of God will help others thrive.

HELP ME, LORD, TO CATCH MYSELF WHEN I START TO CRITICIZE RATHER THAN ENCOURAGE, FROWN INSTEAD OF SMILE, OR TURN AWAY INSTEAD OF REACHING OUT TO HELP. USE ME TO BRING HOPE TO OTHERS.

I AM

But Moses protested, "If I go to the people of Israel and tell them, 'The God of your ancestors has sent me to you,' they will ask me, 'What is his name?' Then what should I tell them?" God replied to Moses, "I AM WHO I AM. Say this to the people of Israel: I AM has sent me to you."

EXODUS 3:13–14 NLT

After God speaks to Moses from the burning bush, Moses asks God for His name. God's reply is simply "I AM." This is not the sort of name that sits quietly on a shelf, requiring no attention, allowing us to take it for granted or forget about it. Basically, God said to Moses that He is Being itself—and not in some remote, abstract kind of way, but in a first-person, present-tense, relational sort of way.

Our personal relationships with this great I AM are the source of all our hope. We can trust that He is ever-present. He is right here with us.

GOD, I CANNOT BEGIN TO FATHOM WHAT YOUR NAME MEANS. I CAN ONLY THANK YOU FOR GIVING ME YOUR ATTENTION, CARE, POWER, AND GRACE—FOR YOUR HOPE-GIVING PRESENCE IN MY LIFE.

Children

"Let the little children come to me, and do not hinder them, for the kingdom of God belongs to such as these."

MARK 10:14 NIV

The children in our lives can be powerful messengers of hope. Usually, if they have grown up surrounded by love, they have not learned yet to dread the future. They experience each moment, each *now*, with their whole heart. They know that there will always be things in life that make them cry, but at the same time, they have no problem believing that life will always be filled with fresh wonders and delights. As we spend time with them, we too can be infected with their joyous curiosity and hope. As Jesus pointed out here in the Gospel of Mark, children just naturally live in the kingdom of God.

Jesus also made clear that we have a responsibility to children to not stand in the way of their coming to Jesus. Adult anger, criticism, and lack of integrity can all squelch a child's hope. As adults, we must be careful to never get in the way of a child's healthy growth, physically, mentally, and spiritually.

THANK YOU, JESUS, FOR EACH CHILD IN MY LIFE.
MAY I LEARN FROM THE JOY, HOPE, AND WONDER
THEY BRING TO EACH DAY—AND MAY I NEVER DO
ANYTHING TO HINDER THEM FROM SEEING YOU.

Worry

*"So don't worry about these things, saying, 'What will
we eat? What will we drink? What will we wear?'...
Seek the Kingdom of God above all else, and live
righteously, and he will give you everything you need."*
MATTHEW 6:31, 33 NLT

One of the great destroyers of hope is worry. Women seem to be especially prone to it. We worry about our children, we worry about our spouses, and we worry about our parents. We also worry what people will think of us; we worry we may have offended someone; we worry about our weight and our appearance; we worry our houses aren't clean enough; we may even worry about those two tiny chin hairs that keep sprouting!

The best strategy for counteracting the worry habit is praying first and allowing God to manage all the things outside our control. Each time our thoughts become tinged with anxiety, we can choose to talk to God instead. It takes effort—old habits are hard to break—but it is well worth it. Prayer will help us focus on God's kingdom as our priority. And prayer can replace our constant worry with a sense of hope.

JESUS, THANK YOU THAT YOU NEVER CONDEMN ME FOR
MY WORRIES. I KNOW THAT, INSTEAD, YOU LONG TO TAKE
THEM FROM ME SO THAT I CAN BE FREE TO EXPERIENCE THE
JOYFUL CERTAINTY OF A HOPE THAT RESTS IN YOU.

Impossible Hope

*"Blessed is she who has believed that the Lord
would fulfill his promises to her!"*
LUKE 1:45 NIV

Elizabeth, the wife of Zechariah and the cousin of Mary, had never been able to have a baby. For a woman of her culture, this was a particularly bitter disappointment. When she was well past the age of being able to get pregnant and had given up all hope of ever becoming a mother, the angel Gabriel came to her husband in the temple and told him that Elizabeth would bear a child. The angel's message came true, and Elizabeth gave birth to the child who would grow up to be John the Baptist. When Elizabeth had given up hope of ever becoming a mother, God used her to tell the world that no situation is ever hopeless. Nothing is impossible with God.

What "impossible" situations are in your life? Instead of allowing them to discourage you and rob you of hope, remember that these may be the very circumstances God wants to use in some surprising way!

LORD, YOU KNOW ALL THE PROBLEMS THAT TO ME SEEM
IMPOSSIBLE TO SOLVE. HELP ME TO GIVE EACH ONE TO YOU,
TRUSTING YOU TO DO WHAT IS BEST IN EACH SITUATION. I
DON'T KNOW WHAT YOU WILL DO, BUT MY HOPE IS IN YOU.

The Door of Hope

"I know your deeds. See, I have placed before you an open door that no one can shut. I know that you have little strength, yet you have kept my word and have not denied my name."

REVELATION 3:8 NIV

In the book of Revelation, Jesus promises the church at Philadelphia that He has new opportunities in store for them. Notice that He doesn't condemn the church for being weak; instead, He praises them for their commitment to Him despite their weakness. We too can lay claim to Jesus' reassurance. Although we are often lacking in strength, Jesus has new doors for us to open, doors that will lead us to amazing vistas and thrilling adventures. He promises that nothing and no one can keep us from walking through those doors. As the apostle Paul knew, when we are at our weakest—and we stop trying to be in control of our own lives and surrender them to God—that is the very moment when God gives us the most strength (2 Corinthians 12:10).

WHEN I FIND MYSELF IN A VALLEY OF TROUBLE, ALL MY STRENGTH GONE, SHOW ME YOUR DOORWAY TO HOPE, LORD JESUS.

Stress

When doubts filled my mind, your comfort
gave me renewed hope and cheer.
PSALM 94:19 NLT

The Hebrew word translated here as "doubt" referred not to intellectual doubt about God but rather to that state of excited anxiety we've all experienced when our thoughts race, our stomachs churn, and our hearts beat hard.

In fact, what the psalmist is describing is what scientists today call the *fight-or-flight response*, when a sense of danger triggers our bodies to prepare to either run away or fight. That response is all well and good when we have to either avoid danger or struggle against it, but most of the time, particularly in our modern world, the dangers we face aren't the sort we can either flee or slug in the nose. Situations like unhappy bosses, troubled marriages, rebellious children, or financial worries create the same response as physical danger, but our bodies' reactions can build up into the destructive condition we call *stress*. No amount of willpower can stop these reactions—but we can find ways to manage our stress more effectively. One way is to seek God's comfort as quickly as possible through praying, reading scripture, or talking to a trusted friend. Although it's unlikely God will remove all stress from our lives, as we renew our hope in Him, we will discover that His joy goes much deeper than our anxiety and stress.

WHEN I'M OVERWHELMED WITH STRESS, LORD,
RENEW MY HOPE AND COMFORT ME.

Never Alone

Now may our Lord Jesus Christ himself and God our Father, who loved us and by his grace gave us eternal comfort and a wonderful hope, comfort you and strengthen you in every good thing you do and say.
2 Thessalonians 2:16–17 nlt

Again and again, the Bible assures us that we are not on our own. As we read these verses, we, along with the church at Thessalonica, can lay claim to Paul's prayer for eternal comfort and a wonderful hope, coming to us directly from Jesus and the Father. What's more, in each thing we do and say (provided we speak and act in love), God is there with us, strengthening us and encouraging us. No matter how discouraged or weak we may feel, we are not alone. We have a coworker and companion whose grace and power are big enough to handle anything we encounter. God's grace gives us the strength for anything we may face.

DEAR HOLY COMPANION, THANK YOU THAT AS WE WORK TOGETHER TO BUILD YOUR KINGDOM, I NEVER HAVE TO FACE ANYTHING ALONE. YOUR POWER AND LOVE UNDERGIRD MY EVERY ACTION AND EVERY WORD, MAKING UP FOR ANY MISTAKES OR WEAKNESSES ON MY PART. WHENEVER I FALTER TODAY, REMIND ME THAT MY HOPE DOES NOT RELY ON MY STRENGTH BUT ON YOURS.

In the Here and Now

So I saw that there is nothing better for people than to be happy in their work. That is our lot in life. And no one can bring us back to see what happens after we die.

ECCLESIASTES 3:22 NLT

What the ancient author of Ecclesiastes writes in this verse is a truth we all must face: this life is the only one we know. We believe in the life to come in eternity with God, but we have never seen or experienced what that life will be like. We also cannot see what will happen in the future; we may never know what the results will ultimately be to many of the projects and causes we hold so dear. We face the future with hope, but at the same time we must find joy and satisfaction in our work in the here and now. Hope is what allows us to surrender to God, allowing Him to hold what lies ahead in His hand, while we do the best we can with the responsibilities He has given us today.

GOD OF PAST, PRESENT, AND FUTURE, GIVE ME THE COURAGE AND HOPE TO WORK HARD FOR YOU TODAY, GIVING MY BEST EFFORT TO BUILDING YOUR KINGDOM, WHILE AT THE SAME TIME I LEAVE THE FUTURE OF MY WORK IN YOUR HANDS.

The Fuel of Hope

Be renewed in the spirit of your mind.
EPHESIANS 4:23 KJV

We all need to be regularly renewed. We are like cars that need to fill up regularly with gas; none of us can keep running on an empty tank. This means that when our supply of hope runs dry, we don't need to feel ashamed or think that God is displeased with us. Instead, we simply must go back to the source of our hope and ask for a new supply.

One way to do this is to spend some time focusing on the good things God has already given us. Each of us has our share of problems, but all of us are also blessed in countless ways. We must turn our attention away from our limitations and instead focus on our blessings!

WHEN DISCOURAGEMENT CREEPS INTO MY THOUGHTS AND EMOTIONS, LORD GOD, REMIND ME TO TURN TO YOU FOR A NEW "TANK" OF HOPE. DON'T LET MY TRIALS AND TRIBULATIONS BLOCK THE SIGHT OF ALL THE JOYS MY LIFE STILL HOLDS.

The Water of Life

"Let anyone who is thirsty come to me and drink."

JOHN 7:37 NIV

If we believe in Christ intellectually, why don't we also believe in Him emotionally? Why do we settle for a life of frustration, irritation, and dejection? The source of all hope is freely available to us; there's no reason not to turn to Him for help and comfort.

In the next couple of verses after this one, John lets us know that Jesus was talking about "living water," and then he explains that Jesus was referring to the Spirit. Why might Jesus have used water as a metaphor for the Holy Spirit? Maybe because all life is dependent on water. Without water, our planet would be a barren rock. Without water, we would not be alive. And the Spirit is just as essential to life as water is. The Spirit is the giver of life, the one who refreshes our hearts and gives us hope. Why go thirsty when there is living water freely available?

SPIRIT OF LIFE, THANK YOU THAT YOU ARE ALWAYS READY AND EAGER TO SATISFY MY THIRST FOR HOPE. REMIND ME THAT IF MY HEART FEELS DRY AND BARREN, ALL I NEED TO DO IS SEEK YOU OUT, AND YOU WILL RESTORE MY LIFE.

ALL Your Hope

*So prepare your minds for action and exercise self-control.
Put all your hope in the gracious salvation that will come
to you when Jesus Christ is revealed to the world.*

1 PETER 1:13 NLT

Notice that little word *all* in this verse. Hope in Christ takes a full commitment of our entire selves. We don't hedge our bets by placing half our hope in Christ and half our hope in ourselves (or anything else), nor do we base our hope on statistical odds that might indicate to us what the future is likely to be.

In this epistle from Peter, he emphasizes that hope and action go together. However, we don't just run around in a frenzy, doing this, that, and the other thing in a desperate, last-ditch effort to save the world. Instead, before we act, we think things through. We prepare ourselves so that we're ready as soon as we hear God's voice telling us where to go.

JESUS, MY HOPE IS ALL IN YOU. PREPARE ME TO DO
YOUR WORK, AND THEN SHOW ME WHAT TO DO AND
SAY TO HELP REVEAL YOU TO THE WORLD.

Grace

"My grace is all you need."
2 Corinthians 12:9 nlt

Hope isn't constantly looking behind it, worrying about the past and what could've been done differently. Hope rests in the knowledge that God's grace is all we need. The Greek word our Bibles translate as "grace" is *charis*, a word that has all these meanings wrapped up in it: favor, kindness, sweetness, joy, delight, generosity, pleasure. The word also contains an additional layer of meaning our English word is missing altogether: the image of God leaning toward us, extending Himself to give Himself away, reaching out to us.

When we begin to understand this full meaning of grace—and when we begin to believe it is real in our own lives—then hope will come more easily to our hearts. Because of grace, we have everything we need for today and all our tomorrows.

GOD OF LOVE, THANK YOU FOR YOUR INFINITE GRACE
THAT IS ALWAYS REACHING OUT TO GIVE ME EVERYTHING
I NEED. I DON'T KNOW WHAT SHAPE YOUR GRACE WILL
TAKE IN MY LIFE, BUT I'M WILLING TO WAIT AND SEE.

Tiredness

*So take a new grip with your tired hands and strengthen your
weak knees. Mark out a straight path for your feet so that those
who are weak and lame will not fall but become strong.*

HEBREWS 12:12–13 NLT

We all have times when we're just plain tired. Our weariness may come from a long stretch of sleepless nights (maybe because of a new baby, a new puppy, or just good old insomnia), a challenging week at work, or a lingering illness that has sapped our energy. Tiredness is not only a physical feeling; it also affects our emotions, making us feel discouraged or tearful. In moments like that, hope is what gives us the incentive to keep going.

Notice also the advice the author of the book of Hebrews gives us in verse 13 (ESV): "straight path. . .so that those who are weak and lame will not fall but become strong." In other words, when you're tired is not the time to attempt a new challenge. If you do, you may cause harm to yourself. Instead, take an easier path and give yourself time to rest and heal.

LORD, WHEN I AM TIRED AND WEAK, MAKE MY
HOPE IN YOU STRONG. LEAD ME ON PATHS THAT
WILL RESTORE MY BODY AND MIND.

The Ladder of Hope

He had a dream in which he saw a stairway resting
on the earth, with its top reaching to heaven, and the
angels of God were ascending and descending on it.

GENESIS 28:12 NIV

Because of a family conflict, Jacob was fleeing his family home, and when he stopped for the night, he was so tired he settled for a stone as a pillow. As he lay down to sleep, he must have been feeling discouraged and afraid. But right there in the middle of his troubles, God gave him a vision that brought new hope to him. He saw that this world was connected to the heavenly realm by a shining ladder, a ladder that the angels used to constantly go back and forth between earth and heaven.

We may never have a dream like Jacob's (and our dreams probably won't be remembered and retold for thousands of years!), but hope is a little like Jacob's ladder: it gives us a new vision of our world, allowing us to glimpse a deeper reality beyond our ordinary lives.

GOD OF JACOB, MAY MY HOPE IN YOU INSPIRE ME TO
BUILD YOUR KINGDOM AMID MY EVERYDAY LIFE.

Everyday Hope

Our help is from the LORD, who made heaven and earth.
PSALM 124:8 NLT

According to the online Oxford dictionary, hope as a noun is "a feeling of expectation and desire for a certain thing to happen," and as a verb, it means to "want something to happen." These meanings equate hope with wishing. When we say, "I hope the sun shines tomorrow," we're saying, "I *wish* the sun would shine tomorrow." But this is not at all the hope that the Bible describes.

Biblical hope relies on the Creator of the universe. It is not a wish but an open-ended certainty that no matter what happens, God will help us through. Even as committed followers of Christ, however, we often settle for the dictionary definition of hope, forgetting that there is another form of hope that is ours. We often wait until we're in trouble before we reach for hope in God. But we don't have to wait for something bad to happen to us. Hope is ours every day.

REMIND ME TODAY, CREATOR, THAT HOPE SHINES FROM WITHIN EVEN THE MOST ORDINARY CIRCUMSTANCES (AS WELL AS THE MOST CHALLENGING ONES). TEACH ME TO DAILY LIVE IN YOUR HOPE.

Hard-Earned Growth

God blesses those who patiently endure testing and temptation.
Afterward they will receive the crown of life that God has promised.
JAMES 1:12 NLT

Here it is again—the promise that hard times can lead to a richer life. This biblical truth has been reaffirmed by psychologists, who have noticed that, after a trauma, many people grow stronger in several ways:

- They become more empathetic and able to not only identify with others' pain but find practical ways to reach out and help.
- Their attention shifts away from material possessions and achievements, while relationships and spirituality become more important to them.
- They turn to their faith for help and grow stronger spiritually.
- They use their experiences to fuel their creativity, whether in art, writing, music, or some other form of creation.
- They realize that they are strong enough to survive future troubles, and they gain the courage for facing trials.

GOD OF BLESSING, MAY MY HOPE IN YOU HELP ME TO GROW EVEN DURING THE HARD TIMES, GIVING ME A RICHER, FULLER LIFE AS WELL AS THE POTENTIAL TO SERVE YOU IN NEW WAYS.

Knowing God

I know whom I have believed, and am convinced that he is able to guard what I have entrusted to him until that day.

2 TIMOTHY 1:12 NIV

When we hope, we make room in our lives for something that is yet unknown. We not only accept but welcome the future, regardless of what it holds. As followers of Christ, we *do* know the source of our hope. The more we get to know Him and the deeper we grow in our relationship with Him, the surer and steadier our hope will be.

In the second half of this verse, Paul (who wrote this letter to Timothy) stresses another aspect of our hope in God: the surrender of our lives and everything they hold into God's hands. Hope in God holds nothing back. Notice that giving something to God isn't the same as throwing it away; instead, God guards each thing we give Him, keeping it far safer than we ever could.

HELP ME, LORD GOD, TO GET TO KNOW YOU MORE
AND MORE DEEPLY. I KNOW I CAN TRUST YOU WITH
EVERYTHING I LOVE, AND SO I GIVE IT ALL TO YOU.

Light in the Darkness

Even the darkness will not be dark to you;
the night will shine like the day.

PSALM 139:12 NIV

Sojourner Truth was someone who knew all about darkness—and all about hope. Born into slavery, she often found her mother weeping for her siblings who had been sold. When Sojourner was nine years old, she was sold to a man who often beat her until she bled. She knew almost nothing about Christianity, but she told all her troubles to her Friend "who lived in the sky."

One day, while talking to this Friend, she realized Someone was there with her, Someone who had also been beaten. She expressed to her Friend that she'd always felt His love but did not know His name. She heard Him respond that He was Jesus.

When Sojourner gained her freedom many years later, she used it to speak out for the rights of both women and black people. Her powerful voice, faith in God, and passion for justice captivated audiences. She stood for hope and light during a time of great darkness.

FRIEND JESUS, MAY MY LIFE SHINE BRIGHT WITH THE
HOPE IN YOU THAT EMPOWERED SOJOURNER TRUTH.

Hope That Stays Alert

*"They waited for me as for showers and drank
in my words as the spring rain."*

JOB 29:23 NIV

In this verse, we are again reminded that hope often involves waiting. The author of Job again directs our attention to the natural world, where the seasons of the year remind us that even the hardest phases of our lives give way to life, as God refreshes us with His Word.

Hope not only lifts our hearts; it also inspires us to be open to opportunities for God's grace to flow into our lives. While hope waits, it stays alert so that it will be ready to take advantage of all the possibilities and potential God brings to our lives, like the life-giving showers of springtime.

KEEP MY MIND AND HEART ALERT, WATCHING FOR WHATEVER
WORK OF GRACE YOU ARE ABOUT TO DO IN MY LIFE, LORD GOD.

Adventuresome Hope

Hezekiah put his whole trust in the GOD of Israel. . . .
And GOD, for his part, held fast to him through all his adventures.
2 KINGS 18:5–6 MSG

A life of hope is also a life of adventure. This doesn't mean we'll necessarily travel down the Nile, climb Mount Everest, or explore the pyramids. Adventures also have the potential to happen every day, amid ordinary life. Adventure leaps into the unknown. It is eager to learn new things, and it requires the willingness to commit to an uncertain outcome with an open heart.

Obviously, an adventuresome spirit and a hopeful spirit have a lot in common! Adventure is open to thinking big; it doesn't place limits on life. It embraces challenges with confidence. It knows that adversity and discomfort can give way to exhilaration and triumph. A sense of adventure brings energy and passion to our days. It makes life interesting!

THANK YOU, GOD, THAT LIFE WITH YOU IS FILLED WITH
ADVENTURE. AND THANK YOU THAT THROUGH ALL MY ADVENTURES,
YOU HOLD ME TIGHT JUST AS YOU DID HEZEKIAH.

Wake Up!

Then Jacob awoke from his sleep and said, "Surely the Lord is in this place, and I wasn't even aware of it!"
GENESIS 28:16 NLT

Sometimes we find ourselves walking through our lives like sleepwalkers. We're meeting our daily responsibilities, going to work, and caring for our homes and families, but we're on autopilot. It's as though something inside us has frozen, and we have no sense of God's presence with us. Feelings like this happen to us all; they're a normal aspect of human experience.

Thankfully, God will send something along to wake us up from our stupor—and then, like Jacob, we'll say, "Oh, God was here with me all along! I just didn't know." God's reality in our lives does not depend on our emotional perceptions.

WAKE ME UP, LORD, SO THAT I CAN ONCE MORE EXPERIENCE
THE HOPE OF YOUR PRESENCE IN MY LIFE.

Renewed

*"Remember that you were slaves in Egypt and that
the LORD your God brought you out of there with
a mighty hand and an outstretched arm."*
DEUTERONOMY 5:15 NIV

When we feel discouraged with our lives today, remembering what God
has done in the past can give us new hope for the future. As we look back
from today's perspective, we can see all the ways God was there with us,
even in our lowest moments, and how He used those moments to lead us
into the promise of new adventures and greater growth.

Then, as we face today's trials with greater hope, we will impart our
future selves with still more memories of God's power in our lives.

LORD GOD, GIVE ME EYES TO SEE YOUR PRESENCE
IN MY PAST SO THAT I HAVE RENEWED HOPE TODAY,
CREATING A LEGACY OF HOPE FOR TOMORROW.

159

Hope for Old Age

*For his sake I have discarded everything else, counting
it all as garbage, so that I could gain Christ.*
PHILIPPIANS 3:8 NLT

Have you ever noticed there are two kinds of old people? One is bitter
and crotchety, while the other has a wise serenity. Since we're all going to
be old people one day (if we're not already!), we might try to understand
why old age can take such different routes.

I wonder if the ability to hope, as well as the ability to let go, isn't the
explanation. Old age asks us all to let go of so many things—physical
strength, professional roles, the sense of our own importance, often eye-
sight or hearing, sexual attractiveness, and sometimes even mental acuity
and memory. The spiritual discipline of old age may be the biggest challenge we'll all face. Yet, if we freely surrender to Christ everything age
takes from us, we may find we have more room in our hearts for the eternal
hope that is ours.

AS I AGE, LORD JESUS, HELP ME NOT TO CLING TO THE MEMORY
OF WHO I ONCE WAS BUT INSTEAD BE FILLED WITH THE
JOYFUL ANTICIPATION OF WHO I AM BECOMING IN YOU.

The Hope of Transformation

"You'll be transformed. You'll be a new person!"
1 Samuel 10:6 MSG

Have you ever read *Hinds Feet on High Places*? It's an allegory about the spiritual life, written in the 1950s by Hannah Hurnard. In the story, Much Afraid travels from the Valley of Humiliation to the high places of the Shepherd. Fear and shame have made her unable to hope, but the Shepherd introduces her to a new image of herself. At first, she believes it's impossible that she will ever be able to surmount her various disabilities and scars. But the Shepherd says to her that He loves to transform wounds and limitations into astounding strengths.

Jesus loves to do amazing, transformative things in our lives. He turns around impossible situations, and He gives butterfly wings to even the most earthbound caterpillars. What astounding thing might He be waiting to do in your life?

SHEPHERD, THANK YOU THAT YOU BELIEVE IN ME. YOU SEE PAST MY FLAWS TO THE PERSON I WAS CREATED TO BE. DAY BY DAY, YOU ARE TRANSFORMING ME, FREEING ME FROM ALL THE OLD SCAR TISSUE THAT HAS HELD ME BACK FOR SO LONG.

Metaphors of Hope

"But as I told you, you have seen me and still you do not believe."
JOHN 6:36 NIV

In these verses, Jesus is speaking with metaphors, as He so often did, comparing Himself to food and water. Our English teachers may have told us not to mix metaphors, but Jesus knew God is too large to be confined to a single analogy. If we said, "God is like a rock and nothing else," we would limit God to the qualities that a rock has—solidity and permanence, for example—but there is far more to God than that.

God nourishes us like food, gives us life like water, sheds light into our lives like the sun, understands us like a friend, adores us like a faithful husband, protects us like a fortress, cares for us like a mother, spreads out through reality like a tree, and unifies us the way a vine connects its branches.

The Bible shows us a God who comes to us in things as ordinary as wind and bread, birds and beasts. Notice that all these metaphors are drawn from the physical world. If we open our eyes and ears, we'll perceive God reflected everywhere.

LORD, MAY EVERY GLASS OF WATER, EVERY BITE OF FOOD,
EVERY BREATH I TAKE ENLARGE MY HOPE IN YOU.

Draw Near to God

Come near to God and he will come near to you.
JAMES 4:8 NIV

When we're feeling swamped with discouragement and emotional weariness, it's always a good idea to look at our lives and see when the last time was that we shut everything else out and focused on God. If He seems far away, there's a pretty good chance we have forgotten to seek Him out. Of course, God hasn't gone anywhere; He's as close to us as ever, surrounding us with His love, but the stress and busyness of daily life can dull our spiritual perception.

When you find yourself in that state, try setting aside a quiet morning, afternoon, or evening (a time when you're not as likely to be interrupted) to spend alone with God. Go for a walk with Him. Read the Bible. Read a book that brings new insight into your spiritual life. Listen to music. Journal. And pray. Take time to catch up with God (and with yourself).

THANK YOU, HEAVENLY FRIEND, THAT YOU ARE ALWAYS
WITH ME, EVEN WHEN I CAN'T FEEL YOUR PRESENCE. MAY
I REMEMBER THAT FEELINGS OF HOPELESSNESS ARE ONLY
REMINDERS THAT I NEED TO SPEND MORE TIME WITH YOU.

God Alone

We have put our hope in the living God,
who is the Savior of all people.
1 TIMOTHY 4:10 NIV

We live immersed in a culture that has a different definition of hope than the one we find in the Bible, so our ideas about hope can easily become warped. Instead of the hope that is the close sibling of trust, which believes God has good things in store for us but allows God to decide what shape those things will take, we start to put demands on our hope. We want to dictate to God the exact things our future should hold. Our focus shifts from God to all the good things this life has to offer. We want to be able to control the form His blessings will take, and when things turn out differently than what we'd "hoped," we may feel angry or betrayed. But when we focus our hope on God alone, He will never disappoint us.

MAY MY HOPE BE IN YOU ALONE, GOD. HELP ME TO BE OPEN
TO WHATEVER YOU SEND INTO MY LIFE. I KNOW YOU WILL
REVEAL YOURSELF TO ME THROUGH BOTH JOY AND SORROW.

The Happy Endings Love Brings

"Love one another. In the same way I loved you, you love one another. This is how everyone will recognize that you are my disciples—when they see the love you have for each other."

JOHN 13:34–35 MSG

Relationships built on love create hope. Friendship creates a space where two people mutually encourage each other, and so should marriage. Divine love also flows through the relationships between parents and children, allowing both sides of the equation to open new possibilities in the world. As we reach out past our close friends and family, seeking to spread love across a wider area, finding practical ways to help and serve, we bring hope to people who are suffering—and our own hearts are encouraged.

We live in a world that was created for community by the triune God. The good news of the restored relationship between God and humanity also allows for better relationships with others here on earth. That is the kind of hope the Bible gives us—and it is the kind of happy-ending story we are called to tell in our lives and in the world around us.

TODAY, FATHER, MAY I WORK WITH YOU TO BUILD THE
HOPE OF HAPPY ENDINGS IN OTHERS' LIVES.

Self-Doubt

Moses pleaded with the LORD, "O Lord, I'm not very good with words. . . . I get tongue-tied, and my words get tangled."
EXODUS 4:10 NLT

Just as we often do, Moses doubted his abilities. When he heard God's calling for his life, he was discouraged before he even began. We've all been there, haven't we? Sometimes, we face challenges we know are just too hard for our skill sets to handle. And that's the moment we realize how much we depend on God.

When Moses voices his discouragement to God, God doesn't try to encourage Moses by saying, "Come on now, your speech problems aren't all that bad." Instead, God says in verses 11 and 12, "Who makes a person's mouth? Who decides whether people speak or do not speak. . . ? Is it not I, the LORD? Now go! I will be with you as you speak, and I will instruct you in what to say." No matter what discouragement we face, we know that, as He did for Moses, God promises to be with us every step of the way and provide the abilities and opportunities we need to fulfill His plan.

FAITHFUL LORD, WHEN I FEEL DISCOURAGED WITH MYSELF,
REMIND ME THAT YOU ARE WITH ME. MY HOPE IS IN YOU.

Blind Hope

*Now faith is confidence in what we hope for and
assurance about what we do not see.*

HEBREWS 11:1 NIV

The Law of Attraction is one of the ideas that's become popular lately (though it's been around since the nineteenth century). It's a belief that whatever can be imagined and held in the mind's eye is achievable. Simply by focusing on a clear mental picture of what we want in life, we will pull whatever it is toward us, making it a reality in our lives.

It's easy to confuse this with the biblical understanding of hope, but once again, we're reminded that our hope and certainty are based only on faith in Christ. We cannot see or even imagine what God has in store for us—but we are certain we can trust Him. We don't need to create an exact picture of the future. Instead, we simply rest in the knowledge that even our smallest acts of love, through the power of divine grace and creativity, somehow contribute to the future of God's kingdom.

REMIND ME, CHRIST, TO LET GO OF MY OWN IDEAS ABOUT THE
FUTURE AND INSTEAD TRUST YOUR CREATIVITY AND GRACE TO
BRING SOMETHING BETTER THAN I COULD EVER IMAGINE.

Each Word a Gift

Say only what helps, each word a gift.
EPHESIANS 4:29 MSG

Our words have tremendous power. That's something the Bible tells us again and again. In fact, it talks more about the danger of careless words than it does about any other kind of sin. And yet it's so easy to forget to be careful with our speech, so tempting to make excuses for gossip, cross words, and criticism. Even when we avoid those pitfalls, our words may be empty of any real meaning, or they may spread pessimism and negativity.

What if we selected our words as carefully as if they were gifts intended for a person we love? What if every single word's goal was to be of positive help? It sounds impossible, doesn't it? But new habits are built one step (one word) at a time—and God will do His part.

LORD OF POSSIBILITY, TEACH ME TO CONSIDER
MY WORDS IN A NEW WAY, AND HELP ME TO FORM
HABITS OF SPEECH THAT GIVE LIFE AND HOPE.

The Kingdom of Heaven

"Your kingdom come, your will be done, on earth as it is in heaven."
MATTHEW 6:10 NIV

These words are so familiar that their meaning may escape us. We say them from habit, without stopping to consider what they ask of us. We are to work and pray that God's kingdom be tangible, as much here in our fallen world as it is in heaven.

Jesus described His Father's kingdom in many ways. It is like scattered seed, He said (Matthew 13:1–9); a wheat field (Matthew 13:14–30); a mustard seed (Matthew 13:31–32); leaven in bread dough (Matthew 13:33); a treasure, a pearl (Matthew 13:44–46); a net (Matthew 13:47–50); and a wedding feast (Matthew 22:2). In other words, God's kingdom is something that starts out small and grows into something larger. It exists within our current reality, hidden like buried treasure, sprinkled like seeds, bubbling like yeast. It is inclusive, as impartial in its vast sweep as a fisherman's net, and as openhearted as a generous host. And it is our job to serve that kingdom.

Hope is the energy that keeps us working for God's kingdom, no matter how dark the world may seem.

SPIRIT, GUIDE ME AND TEACH ME SO THAT I CAN WORK
WITH YOU TO BUILD THE KINGDOM OF HEAVEN.

Light-Bringer

Each one of us needs to look after the good of the people around us, asking ourselves, "How can I help?"

ROMANS 15:2 MSG

As a child, Helen Keller lived in a dark and silent world. Only the persistence and kindness of her teacher were able to bring her out into the world of other human beings, where, despite her total blindness and deafness, she became a famous author, speaker, and political activist. Hope had carried her out of the darkness and helplessness into the light of service and new possibilities.

In the interconnected kingdom of heaven, we all need to look after each other—and when we lend a helping hand to another, our own world is lit with renewed hope. We can be like Helen's teacher, Anne Sullivan, whose heart sang with joy when Helen finally began to understand what was being taught, which opened a new world of possibilities for her. When we look after another person and give them hope, we see the miraculous possibilities in them and in ourselves.

LORD, I ASK THAT YOU GIVE ME THE COURAGE, PERSISTENCE, AND LOVE TO BRING HOPE TO OTHERS' LIVES. IN EVERY RELATIONSHIP AND ENCOUNTER WITH OTHERS, MAY MY ATTITUDE ALWAYS BE "HOW CAN I HELP?" USE ME, I PRAY, TO BRING YOUR LIGHT INTO EVEN THE DARKEST LIVES.

Negative Emotions

I will never forget this awful time, as I grieve over my loss.
Yet I still dare to hope when I remember this: The faithful
love of the LORD never ends! His mercies never cease.

LAMENTATIONS 3:20–22 NLT

If you ever feel as though God condemns you for having negative feelings about your life, read the book of Lamentations. This book in the Old Testament was written in response to the destruction of Jerusalem some six hundred years before Christ. It's full of the emotional ups and downs that come with human life. It records a pattern that most of us will find familiar: we are sunk in despair. . .then we climb up out of our depression and feel more optimistic. . .but something trips us up, and we sink back into our dark hole. . .and then we repeat the entire cycle. Lamentations acknowledges that there is good reason for despair and discouragement—truly terrible things happen in our lives and in the world around us—and yet, because of God's faithful love, we can still find the courage to hope, even amid our human emotions.

LORD, WHEN NEGATIVE EMOTIONS SWAMP ME, MAY
I NEVERTHELESS CLING TO MY HOPE IN YOU.

The Source of Nourishment

*The eyes of all look to you in hope; you give
them their food as they need it.*
PSALM 145:15 NLT

Notice that the psalmist implies that if we want to be nourished, we need to look in the right direction: at God. Focused on our own hunger, we will stay hungry; we need to shift our attention away from our emotions and the situations that have caused them and look instead at the source who can meet our needs.

We would not stare into an empty fridge or pantry just starving ourselves; we would go to the grocery store to stock our shelves and feed ourselves. In the same way, we must look to the Lord for our daily bread. Hope turns our hearts and minds in the right direction, toward the one who will always meet our needs.

WHEN MY HEART FEELS EMPTY, LORD, AND MY SOUL
CRIES OUT FOR NOURISHMENT, REMIND ME THAT
YOU ALONE CAN SUPPLY ME WITH WHAT I NEED.

Choose Hope

Rejoice always, pray continually, give thanks in all circumstances.
1 THESSALONIANS 5:16–18 NIV

How does God expect us to *always* rejoice, pray, and give Him thanks? We've read in other portions of scripture that God understands our negative emotions, and we know that even Jesus experienced sorrow, anger, and fear. So how can we make sense of verses like these?

First, we don't have to be smiling and whistling a cheery tune all the time. (We'd be annoying to those around us if we did!) The Greek word translated as "rejoice" contained wider meanings than simple happiness; it also meant "to thrive," and *HELPS Word-studies* says that it meant to experience and be conscious of God's grace. It's also the same word used in Romans 12:12, which instructs us to "rejoice *in hope*."

In other words, even amid sorrow and anxiety, we can continue to hope, as we also continue to be aware of God's grace. When we make ongoing prayer and gratitude the habitual background of our thought lives, rejoicing in hope becomes possible.

JESUS, I CHOOSE HOPE. SHOW ME HOW TO REJOICE IN THAT HOPE, GIVING THANKS AND PRAYING, EVEN WHEN I'M SAD OR WORRIED.

Gardeners of Hope

Do not exasperate your children; instead, bring them
up in the training and instruction of the Lord.
EPHESIANS 6:4 NIV

God calls us to not only have hope in our hearts but to also teach hope to the children in our lives—and this verse from Paul's letter to the church at Ephesus reminds us that we don't give children hope if we are constantly nagging and scolding them.

The Greek word translated as "instruction" in this version of the Bible had to do with calling attention to something. In other words, our words and actions around children need to help them notice what God is doing in the world. If we're going through a hard time in our lives, we need to be careful not to vent our emotions on our children or allow our negativity to infect their outlooks. God calls us to be like faithful and patient gardeners in the lives of our children, cultivating their lives with love and hope

HELP ME, LORD, TO PLANT SEEDS OF HOPE IN THE
LIFE OF EACH CHILD IN MY LIFE, AND THEN SHOW
ME HOW TO NURTURE AND WATER THOSE SEEDS SO
THAT THEY GROW UP STRONG AND HEALTHY.

Thoughts

We take captive every thought to make it obedient to Christ.

2 CORINTHIANS 10:5 NIV

Psychologists tell us that thoughts have a significant impact on our lives. If our thoughts focus on self-judgment, negativity, and anticipating the worst, those thoughts have the power to shape our behaviors and even our physical health. But our thoughts tell lies, and when we believe those lies, they rob us of the hope we have in Christ. What's more, our negative thoughts can cause us emotional, spiritual, and physical harm.

But when negative thoughts pop up (as they always do), we don't have to automatically surrender to them. We can choose to talk back to them. As Paul wrote in his letter to the Corinthians, we can take our thoughts captive and make them obedient to Christ's message of hope and love.

So, remember—your thoughts are powerful, but you don't have to let them run your life. You can take control by putting your hope in Christ.

TEACH ME, JESUS, TO GIVE YOU CONTROL OVER MY THOUGHT LIFE.
FILL ME, I PRAY, WITH THOUGHTS OF YOUR LOVE AND HOPE.

Eternity in Our Hearts

Yet God has made everything beautiful for its own time. He has planted eternity in the human heart, but even so, people cannot see the whole scope of God's work from beginning to end.

ECCLESIASTES 3:11 NLT

Something inside the human heart insists that this life cannot be all there is. We all long for a world that lasts longer than our short lives. Over the thousands of years that humanity has been around, we've come up with lots of ideas about what eternity is like, but the truth is we just don't know. But not knowing doesn't mean it doesn't exist.

The deep-seated feeling we have is not a lie: Christ promised us a home with Him in eternity. Our longing for deeper purpose and meaning than this life can offer leads us to the one who is the source of our hope.

SOURCE OF ALL HOPE, THANK YOU THAT YOU HAVE A
WORLD OF ENDLESS GOOD IN STORE FOR ME.

Work for the Lord

Whatever you do, work at it with all your heart, as
working for the Lord, not for human masters.

<small>COLOSSIANS 3:23 NIV</small>

In J. R. R. Tolkien's great fantasy, *The Lord of the Rings*, the two hobbits Frodo and Sam have traveled together through many dangers, and now, as they near the end of their journey, they stand staring out at a dark land full of smoke and ruin, where nothing grows. Sam points out all the things that make it seem impossible for them to keep going, but Frodo responds that even when he doesn't see or feel the hope, he must do all that is in his power to do to make the best of it.

That is the attitude Paul is recommending in this verse from his letter to the Colossians. Even when we see no reason to hope, we keep working. We keep taking one faithful step after another. We look past the darkness and danger and work for God and His kingdom. And when, like Frodo and Sam, we refuse to give up, we too, with God's help, will ultimately do the work that has been entrusted to us.

REMIND ME, FAITHFUL GOD, THAT MY WORK IS NOT FOR
MYSELF OR FOR ANY HUMAN, BUT ONLY FOR YOU—AND EVEN
WHEN MY HOPE FAILS ME, YOUR POWER NEVER DOES.

Denial vs. Hope

*If your heart is broken, you'll find G*OD *right there.*
PSALM 34:18 MSG

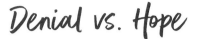

Sometimes, the toughest line for us to draw is the one between hope and denial. At some point, we may look at a particular situation and realize that regardless of all we'd longed for, it just isn't going to change. The chronic disease isn't going to be miraculously healed. The other person in a struggling relationship has given up and we can't change their mind. The dream job we'd hoped for isn't going to be ours. The child we'd hoped would achieve great things is perfectly happy to drift through life. Disappointments like this can break our hearts.

But in situations like these, we need to realize that hope is not the same as denying reality. Instead, we can allow God to bring us to the point of true acceptance and surrender. As we shift perspectives, letting go of the only options we were willing to consider, a range of new possibilities we hadn't previously considered may suddenly become available.

LORD, REMIND ME THAT WHEN YOU PROMISE TO DO THE IMPOSSIBLE, YOU MAY HAVE AN ENTIRELY DIFFERENT PLAN THAN I HAVE IN MIND. MAKE ME OPEN TO WHATEVER YOU WANT TO DO.

Tuned to the Good, the True, and the Beautiful

You can show others the goodness of God, for he called
you out of the darkness into his wonderful light.
1 Peter 2:9 nlt

Peter knew what it was like to be called out of the darkness into the light. When he first became Jesus' disciple, he was impulsive, quick-tempered, and weak. And yet Jesus saw past Peter's flaws to a new identity—the true identity to which God was calling Peter. Jesus even gave him a new name; now he would no longer go by the name Simon, as he had before, but by Peter, which meant "rock." Despite all of Peter's mistakes, this name reflected his true nature. It revealed the hope Jesus had in him.

God calls us to follow Jesus' example when we interact with others. As we see them as Christ sees them, with the eyes of hope, we make room for their real selves to emerge. We can affirm their true identity even if they still haven't claimed it for themselves. We may even help them to see a whole new perspective—God's perspective, the perspective of hope.

GIVE ME YOUR VISION, JESUS, WHEN I LOOK AT
OTHERS IN MY LIFE. TUNE MY AWARENESS TO ALL
THAT IS TRUE, GOOD, AND BEAUTIFUL IN THEM.

A New Dream

Show me the way I should go, for to you I entrust my life.
PSALM 143:8 NIV

When we follow God, trusting Him with our entire lives, we begin to have a new perspective with new values and new dreams. Things we once thought were essential lose their importance, while other things we once considered silly or fanciful take on new substance. The world around us stops looking ordinary and flat, as we perceive the radiance of hope shining through the most everyday features. We begin to see possibilities we never considered before.

But none of this will happen if we insist on holding on to our old values and dreams. We must be open to the new dreams that God is giving us.

THANK YOU, LORD OF POSSIBILITY, THAT YOUR DREAMS FOR ME
ARE FAR GREATER AND MORE BEAUTIFUL THAN ANYTHING I COULD
IMAGINE. I WANT TO READ YOUR NEW STORY FOR MY LIFE.

Silent Prayer

This is the confidence we have in approaching God: that
if we ask anything according to his will, he hears us.

1 John 5:14 niv

We all know that not every prayer is answered, at least not always in the way we'd wanted. Yet, every time we pray and ask God to move in a certain area, we are growing our hope. In this verse, John reminds us that prayer—like hope—requires that we surrender our me-first attitudes and replace them with a whatever-God-wants attitude. This means that prayer should not be just a list of things we want God to do, a long monologue where we seek to tell God what action He should take in the world. Instead, we might better make a prayer habit of first sitting silently in God's presence, asking Him to pray in and through us whatever He is waiting to pray.

So, if you feel tempted sometimes to give up on prayer, when it feels as though you're just talking to empty air, try listening instead of speaking. Allow a silent, wordless hope to fill your time of prayer.

SHOW ME YOUR WILL, LORD GOD. PRAY YOUR PRAYERS
THROUGH ME. REMIND ME THAT ALL MY HOPE IS IN YOU.

The Song of Hope

If all you want is your own way, flirting with the world every chance you get, you end up enemies of God and his way.

JAMES 4:4 MSG

When the Bible speaks of the "world" in verses like this one, it's referring to a system of thinking and living that is not based on hope in God's love. Down through the centuries of history, human societies have always created their own values, placing importance on things like material wealth, power, and fame rather than on the selfless love of Jesus. We easily absorb these values, even when we consider ourselves to be Christ's followers.

That is why James warns us not to "flirt with the world." The world's voice can easily drown out the Spirit's. When that happens, instead of surrendering our lives to God's love, we'll find ourselves right back where we started, with our egos at the center of everything. When we look at the world from this perspective, we often see only frustration and hopelessness. When we surrender to God's way of thinking, however, we can hear the song of hope.

TODAY, SPIRIT, OPEN MY EARS TO YOUR SONG OF HOPE.
TEACH ME TO IGNORE THE WORLD'S VOICE.

When You Fall

Though the righteous fall seven times, they rise again.
PROVERBS 24:16 NIV

Sometimes we talk a lot about sin, encouraging each other to create habits of self-accusation and self-abasement. We may think that these habits would lead us to greater humility and dependence on God, but they are often another way for us to focus on ourselves. This route doesn't lead to hope. Instead, we become chronically disappointed in ourselves—not because we are humble but because we had wanted to excel, and now our pride is wounded.

When we are truly humble, we focus all our attention on God, not on our sins and failures. When we do sin, we accept that we have fallen short of what God wants for us, and we give ourselves anew to Him so that we can go on with fresh hope and confidence in His power and love.

HELP ME, LORD, NOT TO FOCUS ON MY OWN FLAWS
AND MESS-UPS. WHEN I FALL FLAT ON MY FACE,
REMIND ME TO IMMEDIATELY LOOK UP AT YOU.

Courageous Hope

Then she arose with her daughters in law, that she might return from the country of Moab: for she had heard in the country of Moab how that the LORD had visited his people in giving them bread.

RUTH 1:6 KJV

Naomi was originally from Bethlehem, and when her husband died, she wanted to leave the home she had made with him in Moab and go back to her birthplace. She had been gone many years (long enough to raise adult sons), and although there was a famine in Moab, her life there must have been familiar by this time—and yet when she heard that God was helping His people back in her homeland, she went. She didn't just hope that God would miraculously take care of her and her widowed daughters-in-law; she acted.

The Bible is full of stories like Ruth and Naomi's, stories where, with God's help, women found their way against the odds. One daughter-in-law, Orpah, decided to go back to her people, but Naomi and her other daughter-in-law, Ruth, found their way by journeying into the unknown to Bethlehem. There, they found new happiness and security. Ruth, the foreigner, remarried a Jewish man, and she became one of Christ's ancestors.

When Naomi heard a message about what God was doing, she made up her mind and took action. And her determination led to Christ.

GIVE ME THE COURAGE AND HOPE OF NAOMI,
GOD. MAY I GO WHERE YOU LEAD ME.

Fix Your Thoughts

And now, dear brothers and sisters, one final thing.
Fix your thoughts on what is true, and honorable,
and right, and pure, and lovely, and admirable. Think
about things that are excellent and worthy of praise.

PHILIPPIANS 4:8 NLT

Hope in God is easily eroded. It gets washed away in the onslaught of negativity that we read and hear every day. Here again, though, the Bible asks us to take responsibility for our thoughts.

Instead of dwelling on all that is cruel and unfair in the world, look for glimpses of God's justice and truth. Instead of focusing on all the things that irk you in another person, focus on seeing what is admirable in them. And most of all, instead of constantly pondering all that is wrong with yourself—all your failures and your flaws—look at yourself through God's eyes, seeing your own loveliness and potential. Focus on what lies ahead in hopeful expectation.

MAY MY THOUGHTS BE FIXED ON YOUR VISION FOR ME
AND FOR THE WORLD AROUND ME, DEAR LORD.

Shalom

"May they have abundant peace, both near and far," says the LORD, who heals them.

ISAIAH 57:19 NLT

The English definition of peace, according to the online Oxford dictionary, is "freedom from disturbance." The Hebrew word for peace—*shalom*—has a far deeper and more positive meaning, one that's not limited to the political world (as in the absence of war) or the social world (as in the absence of quarrels and disagreements). The Bible's concept of peace describes the reality that God is constantly calling into being, the kingdom of heaven. The word *shalom* contained all these meanings: completeness, safety, well-being, health, prosperity, contentment, friendship, wholeness, and perfection. *Shalom* is the concrete embodiment of our hope in God.

LORD, I WANT TO WORK WITH YOU TO CREATE YOUR SHALOM
IN THE WORLD AROUND ME. HELP ME TO FIX ALL MY
ATTENTION AND EFFORT ON THIS HOPE I HAVE IN YOU.

Justice

"Be just and fair to all. . . . For I am coming soon to rescue
you and to display my righteousness among you."
ISAIAH 56:1 NLT

This verse links justice to the hope we have that God will rescue us from our troubles. Justice is an aspect of God's nature, and it is also something He expects of us. This doesn't mean, though, that we are to judge and punish others. Typically, our concept of justice focuses on two questions: What law was broken? What punishment does the offender deserve? God's justice, however, focuses more on restoration than punishment. It asks: Who has been harmed? What do they need to be healed? What action can we take to bring that healing? This is the kind of justice God calls us to work for. It asks that we become sensitive to others' situations rather than focusing only on our problems and those of our immediate circle. It extends our vision of hope out into the communities around us. Humbly, patiently, we do whatever we can—and then we leave the rest to God.

MAY MY VISION OF HOPE, LORD, GIVE ME THE ENERGY TO WORK
FOR JUSTICE FOR ALL WHO ARE OPPRESSED AND SUFFERING.

Come, Lord Jesus

He who testifies to these things says, "Yes, I am
coming soon." Amen. Come, Lord Jesus.
REVELATION 22:20 NIV

❈

This verse comes at the end of Revelation, the last book in the Bible. The Bible's story ends with this promise—Jesus is coming soon—and our response should be "Yes! Come, Lord Jesus." As we affirm our willingness for Jesus to come, we are not speaking only of the end of time; we are saying we want Jesus to come now, come today, come into our world through us and in us. We are welcoming Him into our lives.

In this world, even the happiest stories end, but in the kingdom of heaven, where Jesus is always coming soon, there are no endings. As followers of Christ, that is the reality in which we live. Because of Jesus, hope goes on forever, a world without end. Amen.

JESUS, COME TODAY INTO MY LIFE. TELL YOUR
NEVER-ENDING STORY OF HOPE THROUGH ME AND IN ME.

Scripture Index

More Blessings for Your Beautiful Heart

978-1-63609-283-6
Flexible Casebound

978-1-63609-396-3
Flexible Casebound

These lovely devotionals are beautiful reminders that blessings abound for women of faith. Each page features an encouraging devotional reading rooted in biblical truth and a heartfelt prayer to help you begin your daily quiet time with the heavenly Father. You will discover all the ways God blesses you every single day as you grow closer to Him and wrap your soul in His unconditional love.

Find This and More from Barbour
Publishing at Your Favorite Bookstore
www.barbourbooks.com

BARBOUR
PUBLISHING